T0328637

Cambridge Elements

Elements in Bioethics and Neuroethics
edited by
Thomasine Kushner
California Pacific Medical Center, San Francisco

PATHOGRAPHIES OF MENTAL ILLNESS

Nathan Carlin
McGovern Medical School

CAMBRIDGE
UNIVERSITY PRESS

Shaftesbury Road, Cambridge CB2 8EA, United Kingdom

One Liberty Plaza, 20th Floor, New York, NY 10006, USA

477 Williamstown Road, Port Melbourne, VIC 3207, Australia

314–321, 3rd Floor, Plot 3, Splendor Forum, Jasola District Centre, New Delhi – 110025, India

103 Penang Road, #05–06/07, Visioncrest Commercial, Singapore 238467

Cambridge University Press is part of Cambridge University Press & Assessment, a department of the University of Cambridge.

We share the University's mission to contribute to society through the pursuit of education, learning and research at the highest international levels of excellence.

www.cambridge.org
Information on this title: www.cambridge.org/9781009073660

DOI: 10.1017/9781009064866

First published 2022

A catalogue record for this publication is available from the British Library.

ISBN 978-1-009-07366-0 Paperback
ISSN 2752-3934 (online)
ISSN 2752-3926 (print)

Pathographies of Mental Illness

Elements in Bioethics and Neuroethics

DOI: 10.1017/9781009064866
First published online: September 2022

Nathan Carlin
McGovern Medical School

Author for correspondence: Nathan Carlin, nathanscarlin@gmail.com

Abstract: This Element is a survey of the field of pathographies of mental illness. It explores classic texts in the field as well as other selected contemporary memoirs. In doing so, the reader is introduced to psychiatric information about various mental illnesses through a narrative lens, emphasizing experience. Because clinical research is evidenced based and aims to produce generalizable knowledge (i.e., trends), the reading of pathographies can complement these findings with practical experiential insights. By pairing psychiatric information with pathographies, certain personal themes become apparent that are different from the empirical trends identified by scientific and medical researchers. Based on the survey presented here, this Element identifies seven such themes, laying the foundation for future research, inquiry, practice, and policy.

Keywords: memoir, pathography, mental illness, narrative

ISBNs: 9781009073660 (PB), 9781009064866 (OC)
ISSNs: 2752-3934 (online), 2752-3926 (print)

Contents

1 Introduction   1

2 What Is Pathography?   2

3 Depression   5

4 Bipolar Disorder   8

5 Schizophrenia   12

6 Addiction   16

7 Borderline Personality Disorder   21

8 Conduct Disorder   25

9 Antisocial Personality Disorder   29

10 Autism Spectrum Disorder   33

11 Eating Disorders   37

12 Key Personal Themes in Pathographies of Mental Illness   40

Appendix: Further Reading   45

Notes   47

References   52

1 Introduction

The purpose of this Element is to offer a survey of the field of pathographies of mental illness. Despite being one of the largest areas of pathography,[1] a foundational survey has not been written – until now.[2] In doing so, this Element will focus on a substantial number of major mental illnesses, including depression, bipolar disorder, schizophrenia, substance use disorders, borderline personality disorder, conduct disorder, antisocial personality disorder, autism spectrum disorder, and eating disorders.

A distinguishing feature of this Element is that it will pair material from the *Diagnostic and Statistical Manual of Mental Disorders* (*DSM*)[3] with classic or contemporary pathographies of mental illness. The language and findings of the *DSM* are the result of tens of thousands of scientific studies, with large data sets, while the episodes recounted in a given pathography are the result of introspective reflection (N = 1). A central claim here is that both of these forms of knowledge – evidence and experience – are valuable. If scientific evidence points to key trends (i.e., findings) with regard to a particular mental illness, which are necessary for diagnosis, pathographies lift up common themes (i.e., insights), which can be useful for treatment and policy.

It is worth pointing out that pathographies, both because they are a snapshot in time and also because they tend to be written by patients, can sometimes present misleading, outdated, or incorrect clinical information. This is another reason why it is important to pair pathographies with the most recent version of the *DSM*. The fact that the *DSM* has undergone many revisions underscores that what we understand mental illness to be is socially and historically conditioned. Like pathographies, all versions of the *DSM* are snapshots in time, reflecting the scientific thinking of a particular moment, also embedding assumptions about race, gender, and other cultural considerations.

In this Element, there will be an emphasis on the classic texts in the field, which leads to a limitation – namely, most of these books have been written by wealthy, educated, White persons. As Meri Nana-Ama Danquah observes in *Willow Weep for Me*, her pathography on depression:

> I have noticed that the mental illness that affects White men is often characterized, if not glamorized, as a sign of genius, a burden of cerebral superiority, artistic eccentricity – as if their depression is somehow heroic. White women who suffer from mental illness are depicted as idle, spoiled, or just plain hysterical. Black men are demonized and pathologized. Black women with psychological problems are certainly not seen as geniuses. . . . When a Black woman suffers from a mental disorder, the overwhelming opinion is that she is weak.[4]

Still, few persons of color have written pathographies. For some mental illnesses, there are none. To somewhat mitigate this bias, an appendix is offered of more recent pathographies with an emphasis on persons of color.

The structure that follows is straightforward, beginning with a discussion of the genre of pathography and then focusing on various mental illnesses, pairing, as noted, pathographies with *DSM* material. In each case, attention is called to the way in which the pathography sheds light on or concretizes clinical criteria, providing a richer understanding of the criteria and illness. In conclusion, key personal themes are offered that cut across the pathographies, demonstrating the value of reading this kind of material for practical use.

2 What Is Pathography?

In medical humanities, the classic text on pathography is Anne Hunsaker Hawkins's *Reconstructing Illness*.[5] She describes the book as "a study of the myths, attitudes, and assumptions that inform the way we deal with illness."[6] Her method is to analyze autobiographies and biographies of illness to make recommendations about contemporary clinical practice. Thus, Hawkins takes pathographies to be autobiographies and biographies of illness – in other words, narratives of illness: path (= illness) + graphy (= narrative). As medical humanities has developed, what has been understood as pathography in terms of genre has broadened (especially with the development of graphic medicine[7]) in that pathography now includes, but consists of more than, narrative.

Of note, Hawkins points out that her own personal experience led her to this area. While she was writing a dissertation on spiritual autobiographies, her father suffered a ruptured cerebral aneurysm that left him partially paralyzed. Impacted by her father's situation, she became interested in the accounts of other people's experiences of illness. Hawkins was particularly moved by Oliver Sacks's *Awakenings*,[8] and it was in this book that she first encountered the word "pathography."[9] When Sacks used the term, he cited Sigmund Freud.[10] As she continued reading pathographies while also doing her graduate work, Hawkins began to wonder "if contemporary pathographies, like the spiritual autobiographies [she] studied, revealed significant truths about the cultures and value systems from which they sprang."[11]

After graduate school, in 1990, Hawkins joined the Humanities Department at the Pennsylvania State University College of Medicine, where she found that her work had a new practical dimension. Her students and colleagues assumed that the study of literature could make medical students into better doctors, an assumption that she came to endorse: "It is in restoring the patient's voice to the medical enterprise that the study of pathography has its greatest importance and offers its greatest promise. . . . It is surely no accident that the appearance of pathography coincides with the triumph of scientific technological medicine."[12] She adds: "Pathographies make such problems vividly and immediately real for us, and thus they have a significant part to play in the movement towards a patient-centered medicine."[13]

In a follow-up essay to her book, Hawkins points out that while the writing of pathographies is, for the most part, a phenomenon that begins in the twentieth century, an early example can be observed in John Donne's seventeenth-century *Devotions Upon Emerging Occasions*, where he explores his experience of illness, from diagnosis to recovery. She adds that, throughout history, there are other examples of pathography-like material that include descriptions of illness, but few take the author's own experience as the central subject, the key characteristic of contemporary pathographies.[14]

Hawkins notes that *Reconstructing Illness*, as a scholarly text, is a metapathography. That is, if pathographies are narratives of illness, she is offering an analysis of these narratives. Her basic argument is that contemporary pathographies tend to fall into three narrative patterns: journey, battle, and rebirth.[15] Hawkins offered other categories elsewhere.[16]

In a review of Hawkins's *Reconstructing Illness*, Arthur Frank, who himself wrote a classic pathography in medical humanities,[17] picks up on the question of truth. He asks: Is the idea that the case reports written by doctors are false but the pathographies written by patients are true? No, quoting Hawkins, Frank writes: "each one distorts, each one tells the truth."[18] Although generally praising Hawkins, Frank concludes by noting that he wishes Hawkins would have provided "a unifying meta-myth" of pathographies, even though he realizes that it was not her intention. Instead, out of respect for patients, she wanted them to be heard in their own voices. Frank writes: "Here is a central dilemma in scholarship about both the experience of illness and medical ethics. If the ethical commitment is to allow ill persons their own voices, how does one write about these voices without appropriating them?"[19] Frank would continue to work on this question in subsequent publications.[20]

Although the most common genre of pathography is memoir, poetry is another important medium for conveying experiences of illness. In "Patient Poets: Pathography in Poetry," Marilyn McEntyre notes that while a great deal of attention has been given to narrative medicine, "poetry opens a very different window from narrative, emphasizing discontinuity, surprise, experiential gaps, and the uneasy relationship between words and the life lived in the body."[21] She adds that poetry teaches us to read and listen differently, emphasizing that "[i]t can be hard to remember that life is not 'story,'" for "things do not happen in sequences or well-constructed plot lines."[22]

In explaining what poetry adds to pathography, McEntyre says: "We can learn to attend to their images, their puzzling line breaks, their shifts of focus – to all the techniques we call 'literary' – as keys to conditions of body and mind that could not be adequately articulated in any more discursive way."[23] McEntyre affirms that "[s]uffering is a truth that must be told 'slant,' as Emily Dickinson advised," adding that "[i]t can be conveyed, but not in simple declarative sentences, and not on scales of one to ten."[24] McEntyre also suggests that poems have practical/clinical value because "everyone who speaks encodes. All dialogue has its pauses, metaphoric detours, apparent irrelevancies, subtexts, allusiveness."[25] She continues: "Reading them well is praxis, and practice for the challenging, subtle, peculiar, rewarding work of reading what is inscribed in the human faces and voices and bodies that come into our clinics and classrooms in the hope of being healed."[26]

2.1 Narrative Ethics

Before moving on to the subject of this Element – the voices of illness as recorded in pathography – a brief discussion is needed to distinguish the field from that of narrative ethics. Narrative ethics is broader than medical ethics, as its concerns include but are beyond medicine. A critical mass of scholarship on narrative ethics within medicine began to appear by the early 2000s. In *Stories Matter*, Rita Charon and Martha Montello offer an edited volume (published in 2002) of key thinkers who helped to establish narrative ethics within and alongside bioethics, medical humanities, literature and medicine, and more. They write: "Narrative ethics arose as doctors, nurses, ethicists, and patients found themselves taking seriously their acts of reading, writing, and telling. From patients' pathographies and caregivers' stories from practice to ethicists' written cases, what unified these early efforts was the recognition of the centrality of narrative in the work of health care."[27] So, the genre of pathography predates – and also helped to establish – narrative ethics within medical circles.

What is narrative ethics? Charon and Montello note that, in their volume, there is not a codified list of propositions that define narrative ethics. Rather, they offer a number of "exemplars" that display what has been called "a narrativist turn" in various fields that recognizes "the extent to which perceptions are embedded in their telling, realizing human beings' reliance on storytelling to get their bearings in life, and acknowledging the innately narrative structure of human knowledge and provisional truth."[28]

In a subsequent essay, Montello described narrative ethics as focusing on *how* people come to particular moral decisions as distinguished from *what* moral decisions they make. Drawing on Martha Nussbaum, Alasdair MacIntyre, and Rebecca Goldstein, Montello refers to this focusing on *how* as exploring the "mattering maps" of people. Mattering maps are "a projection of its inhabitants' perceptions . . . [of] what matters to [a person], what matters overwhelmingly."[29] Montello adds that what matters to different people in the same situation can vary greatly, as can what matters to a person over the course of their lifetime. Therefore, what makes narrative ethics different from, say, usual applications of principlist bioethics is that narrative ethics pays much more attention to issues such as context and emotions.

After defining and describing what pathographies are, and how they differ from narrative ethics, an important question arises: In addition to providing interesting reading, "Why do pathographies matter?" Proposed reasons can be associated with different groups:

- *Authors*: Any serious illness is psychologically as well as physically traumatizing. Organizing what seems to be a chaotic experience into a structured written expression can help to facilitate a sense of control and personal insight. Pathographies matter because they help sufferers make sense of their illness.
- *General Readers*: For those sharing the same condition as the author, the recognition of a similar experience helps to cut through feelings of isolation. Also, the anecdotal perspective can provide general information on the course and treatments of particular illnesses. Pathographies matter because they can provide a practical and existential road map for others.
- *Health Care Professionals*: As unique "windows" into the patient's medical encounters, pathographies can provide insights that would otherwise remain hidden. Pathographies matter because they can prompt self-reflection among doctors, nurses, and others, providing an important tool for improving patient care.

We now turn to examples of pathographies of mental illness and the ways in which they illustrate the descriptions of mental illness found in the *DSM*.

3 Depression

3.1 Darkness Visible

Depression is probably the most well-known mental illness, for it seems to be the most relatable. Who has not felt sadness from time to time? But depression is also often misunderstood because sadness is not depression.

In *Darkness Visible,* William Styron, one of the most influential American fiction writers of the twentieth century, writes about his own depression, near suicide, and hospitalization. A key objective of the book is to destigmatize suicide. Through his own experience, Styron proposes that when people die by suicide, this is not because they are weak, selfish, or immoral. Rather, it is because of pain. Because the pain is so intense and so unrelenting, they see no other option.

Styron suggests that depression is not merely feeling down or "the blues." It is a much more active experience. "For me," he writes, "the pain is most closely connected to drowning or suffocation."[30] He adds:

> It may be more accurate to say that despair, owing to some evil trick played upon the sick brain by the inhabiting psyche, comes to resemble the diabolical discomfort of being imprisoned in a fiercely overheated room. And because no breeze stirs this caldron, because there is no escape from this smothering confinement, it is entirely natural that the victim begins to think ceaselessly of oblivion.[31]

Most people suffering from depression have difficulty sleeping and eating, finding it hard to get out of bed in the morning. Styron, too, had difficulty sleeping, but his depression grew worse as the day progressed, characterized by a mounting stifling anxiety. Other common symptoms (all experienced by Styron) include the inability to concentrate, the loss of rational thought and perspective, confusion, memory problems, panic, difficulty speaking, loss of libido, and an inability to experience pleasure or joy.

What caused Styron's depression? Why did it happen when it did? Styron thinks that such questions really do not have answers and that the best that one can do – for oneself and for others – is to engage in "wise conjecture."[32] In his own case, Styron thinks that his depression was multifactorial: relating to his genetics, the death of his mother while he was a teenager, unhappiness with his writing, turning age sixty, and, perhaps most significantly, his experience of alcohol withdrawal. For decades, Styron would drink throughout the day, in an attempt to calm his anxiety. Drinking also seemed to help his creative process. But his stomach condition forced him to quit drinking – and this might be thought of as the trigger that initiated his depression.

How did Styron improve? He was critical of medication and therapy, but, strikingly, he was very positive about his stay in a psychiatric hospital. He felt that it was time that healed him – not medication or therapy – and that what he needed most was a safe place to be. This contrasts significantly with the negative image of psychiatric hospitals in films (based on books) such as *One Flew Over the Cuckoo's Nest*[33] as well as *Girl, Interrupted,*[34] which depict psychiatric hospitals as oppressive. For Styron, although the hospital was not a luxurious interlude, and while he found parts of it annoying (e.g., therapeutic activities), it nevertheless was a profoundly positive experience for him.

As Hawkins noted, no pathography offers an unfiltered vision of truth. They offer, to use her term, "formulations,"[35] as these narratives are crafted for publication. Another way of saying this is that they offer a perspective. This is demonstrated strikingly in a brief reflection written by Rose Styron, William Styron's wife. According to William, it was his idea to go to the psychiatric hospital, but this does not coincide with Rose's recollection. Rose includes notes from their daughter, Polly, who was with them that night, and these notes were written down shortly after the events unfolded:

> So, I guess I should write this down, or I won't believe it. I came to the house Friday evening because I heard that Dad had had a terrible night on Thursday and that he and Mum were fairly shaken. I was prepared for a morbid gloom, but not for what the night actually turned out to be. When I went upstairs to his room he was lying there, with his long gray hair all tangled and wild. I took his hand, which was trembling. "I'm a goner, darling," he said, first thing. His eyes had a startled look, and seemed to be not quite there. His cool, trembling hands kept fumbling over mine. "The agony's too great now, darling. I'm sorry. I'm a goner." ... He raved about his miserable past and his sins and the waste of his life and how, when they published the scandal of his life, we should try not to hate him. ... "You'll hate me for what I am going to do to myself. My head is exploding. I can't stand the agony anymore." ... When Mum finally came upstairs, as he held me next to him with his eyes closed, I mouthed the word "HOS-PIT-AL to her."[36]

This is very different from William's account; he emphasizes his own strength and initiative in deciding to go to the hospital. But, as a reader, taking into account his daughter's notes of the events recorded so soon after they happened, the perspectives of Rose and Polly seem more compelling. This raises the question: Why did William write the account the way he did? Also, William does not mention a subsequent relapse. Why? Was he trying to serve as an inspiration to others? Was he ashamed? Was he trying to nurture agency among persons suffering from depression? What are the ethical and moral responsibilities of representation?

3.2 Clinical Information

The *DSM-5-TR* has a section on depressive disorders, which includes major depressive disorder. The diagnostic criteria for major depressive disorder include five or more of the following symptoms during the same two-week period:

1. Depressed mood
2. Diminished pleasure and interest

3. Significant weight loss or weight gain
4. Insomnia or hypersomnia
5. Psychomotor agitation or retardation
6. Fatigue
7. Feelings of worthlessness or excessive guilt
8. Diminished ability to concentrate or make decisions
9. Recurrent thoughts of death or suicidal ideation or plans[37]

To make this diagnosis, one of the symptoms must be either depressed mood or loss of pleasure or interest. Also, the symptoms must cause distress or impairment, must not be attributed to another medical condition or substance, and cannot be better explained by another psychiatric disorder. There must never have been a manic or hypomanic episode, unless that episode can be attributed to the use of a substance, medication, or other medical condition.[38]

Styron clearly experienced most of the clinical criteria for major depressive disorder. Symptoms that stood out were diminished pleasure and interest, recurrent thoughts of suicide, excessive guilt for wishing to die by suicide (e.g., "You'll hate me for what I am going to do!"), and diminished ability to concentrate, resulting in the loss of his ability to work productively, which was so central to his identity.

A key claim of *Darkness Visible* is that depression cannot be understood by persons who have not experienced it, that it is a sui generis experience. If, for example, a person is color-blind and they cannot see the color yellow, there is no way to describe the color of a lemon to them, for yellow cannot be described in any other terms. And this is what Styron thinks depression is like: If you have not experienced it, you just cannot understand it. This is underscored in the pathography when Styron describes his interactions with his psychiatrist, especially with his disbelief as to his psychiatrist's inability to understand his complete lack of libido.

It is one thing to know the clinical criteria for depression; it is another to understand how the illness is experienced in a depressed person's life. Although some of the material in *Darkness Visible* is dated – for example, the cultural stigma associated with depression is no longer the same as it was when Styron was writing – what Styron gives us, as a professional writer, is the gift of a description of an inner experience that is almost not understandable by outsiders.

4 Bipolar Disorder

4.1 An Unquiet Mind

Like Styron's *Darkness Visible*, Kay Redfield Jamison's *An Unquiet Mind* is an acclaimed classic among pathographies of mental illness, and a highly recommended resource in the literature of bipolar illness. Although depression is a condition more commonly found relatable, experiences of mania or psychosis are less so. A layperson asked to describe the symptoms of bipolar illness would typically have difficulty in doing so. Sometimes the words "borderline" and "bipolar" are confused, as there is a tendency to incorrectly associate borderline with being manic, which is often a symptom of bipolar disorder. Also, borderline is a personality disorder, while bipolar is a mood disorder.

Like Styron, Jamison has led a very productive life because of her socioeconomic class and strong social connections. Although she considered going to medical school, she instead chose graduate school in order to study clinical psychology. Jamison correctly intuited that the structure of medical education was too rigid for her. However, despite having studied the illness, her insight during the early years of its manifestations was limited. Even when she did concede that she was ill, she resisted treatment because, in part, she saw the illness as "an extension of myself."[39] She writes:

> My manias, at least in their early and mild forms, were absolutely intoxicating states that gave rise to great personal pleasure, an incomparable flow of thoughts, and a ceaseless energy that allowed the translation of new ideas into papers and projects. Medications not only cut into these fast-flowing, high-flying times, they also brought with them seemingly intolerable side effects. It took me far too long to realize that lost years and relationships cannot be recovered.[40]

Because Jamison worked as a professor at a medical school, some of her manic episodes were extremely beneficial, as she could write a journal article in a single night, making it easy for her to produce enough publications for tenure. There were downsides too. Sometimes, when she was on medication, she was not able to read because of side effects. This caused her a great deal of suffering because her intellectual life was so central to her identity.

Most pathographies tend to offer lessons learned – often about the importance of therapy or medication – and Jamison creatively conveyed her own such lessons by creating a list of "Rules for the Gracious Acceptance of Lithium into Your Life":

1. Clear out the medicine cabinet before guests arrive for dinner or new lovers stay the night.
2. Remember to put the lithium back into the cabinet the next day.
3. Don't be too embarrassed by your lack of coordination or your inability to do well the sports you once did with ease.

4. Learn to laugh about spilling coffee, having the palsied signature of an eighty-year-old, and being unable to put on cuff links in less than ten minutes.

5. Smile when people joke about how they think they "need to be on lithium."

6. Nod intelligently, and with conviction, when your physician explains to you the many advantages of lithium in leveling out the chaos in your life.

7. Be patient when waiting for this leveling off. Very patient. Reread the Book of Job. Continue being patient. Contemplate the similarity between the phrases "being patient" and "being a patient."

8. Try not to let the fact that you can't read without effort annoy you. Be philosophical. Even if you could read, you probably wouldn't remember most of it anyway.

9. Accommodate to a certain lack of enthusiasm and bounce that you once had. Try not to think about all the wild nights you once had. Probably best not to have had those nights anyway.

10. Always keep in perspective how much better you are. Everyone else certainly points it out often enough, and, annoyingly enough, it's probably true.

11. Be appreciative. Don't even *consider* stopping your lithium.

12. When you do stop, get manic, get depressed, expect to hear two basic themes from your family, friends, and healers:

   ◦ But you were doing so much better, I just don't understand it.
   ◦ I told you this would happen.

13. Restock your medicine cabinet.[41]

This list, while sad and humorous, captures many of the practical difficulties of living with bipolar illness.

4.2 Clinical Information

In the *DSM-5-TR*, there is a section on bipolar and related disorders. It is between the section on depressive disorders and the section on schizophrenia spectrum and other psychotic disorders, recognizing that bipolar disorders are "a bridge between the two diagnostic classes in terms of symptomology, family history, and genetics."[42]

The focus here is on bipolar I. To make this diagnosis, there must be at least one manic episode. A manic episode involves an abnormally elevated, expansive, or irritable mood, along with increased energy or activity, lasting for at least a week. During this period, there must be three (or more) of the following symptoms (or four if the mood is only irritable):

1. Grandiosity
2. Decreased need for sleep
3. Unusually talkative
4. Racing thoughts
5. Distractibility
6. Increase in goal-directed activity (e.g., many work projects)
7. Excessive involvement in risky activities, especially involving finances and sexual behavior[43]

This manic episode must cause impairment in social or work relationships, include a risk of hurting self or others, or have psychotic features. Also, this mood disturbance cannot be attributed to another medical or psychiatric condition or the effects of a substance or medication.[44]

A hypomanic episode is less severe than a manic episode; it does not require hospitalization. Also, there are not psychotic features in hypomania. Bipolar I can, and often does, include major depressive episodes, as described earlier, but bipolar I does not require the experience of a major depressive episode. A striking feature of bipolar disorder is that lifetime suicide risk is "20-to 30-fold greater than in the general population."[45]

Jamison conveys her experience of bipolar (especially as distinguished from depression) very clearly. Some of her symptoms that stand out are decreased need for sleep (as noted by colleagues), racing thoughts (as observed by friends), increase in goal-directed activity (as indicated by number of work projects), and excessive involvement in risky activities (as evidenced by her self-inflicted financial problems). It is worth noting that Jamison's financial problems were only solvable because of her supportive family.

From her pathography, a key feature worth highlighting is how Jamison writes so positively about her mania, how pleasurable it was. And, when hypomanic, her increased ability toward goal-directed activity was very helpful to her professionally. In this regard, among the most quoted lines from the book are in the epilogue:

> I have often asked myself whether, given the choice, I would choose to have manic-depressive illness. If lithium were not available to me, or didn't work for me, the answer would be a simple no – and it would be an answer laced with terror. But lithium does work for me. ... Strangely enough, I think I would choose to have it.[46]

She goes on to note that depression is terrible and that there is nothing good about it, except perhaps that one might be able to better empathize with others who have experienced it. In any case, Jamison believes that her mania has given her a life richer than she otherwise could have had: "I have felt more things, more deeply; had more experiences, more intensely; loved more, and been more loved; laughed more often for having cried more often; appreciated more the springs, for all the winters."[47]

This issue could be called: *The Jamison Question*. In other words, if it were possible to prevent or cure a given disease, should we? This raises a question in the philosophy of medicine generally and in goals of psychiatry research specifically: Should we attempt to eliminate bipolar disease? Since clinical criteria need to cause personal or social distress or impairment, what do we do when patients claim that their symptoms are enhancements? As we will see, other writers pick up on *The Jamison Question* and answer it in their own way.

5 Schizophrenia

5.1 The Center Cannot Hold

Elyn Saks's *The Center Cannot Hold* pairs nicely with Jamison's *An Unquiet Mind*. Both titles offer key firsthand images of mental illness: A person suffering from bipolar has a mind that is "unquiet," while a person suffering from schizophrenia does not have an organized ego (a center that "holds").

The central message of *The Center Cannot Hold* is hope, an element that for Saks is important to stress because it is often believed that the disease is neurodegenerative (there is reason to doubt that it is[48]) and that, if a person suffers from schizophrenia, their life cannot be meaningful (this is not true). Also, people tend to associate schizophrenia with homelessness, institutionalization, and serious crime.[49] But persons suffering from serious mental illness such as schizophrenia are usually more likely to be a danger to themselves than to others.[50]

A striking feature about the Saks pathography is that she does not fit the popular image of persons suffering from schizophrenia; she has been extremely successful, having graduated from Vanderbilt University, Oxford University, and Yale Law School. Saks grew up in suburban northern Miami and describes her family as "somewhat observant" Jews.[51] A middle-class family, her father had a law practice that dealt primarily with real estate. Her mother was a stay-at-home mom. She notes that she had a good childhood with vacations and no real financial concerns.

When Saks was eight years old, she developed some quirks (such as obsessive handwashing) and also began to have night terrors, fearing that someone might break in through her window. She recalls one particular memory from around this time. Her father snapped at her for interrupting his work, and after this reprimand:

> Something odd happens. My awareness (of myself, of him, of the room, of the physical reality around and beyond us) instantly grows fuzzy. Or wobbly. I think I am dissolving. I feel – my mind feels – like a sand castle with all the sand sliding away in the receding surf. *What is happening to me? This is scary, please let it be over!* I think maybe if I stand very still and quiet, it will stop.[52]

She comments that when she tries to explain the experience to others, people can understand the feeling of being afraid but they have difficulty understanding the experience of disorganization:

> Consciousness gradually loses its coherence. One's center gives way. The center cannot hold. The "me" becomes a haze, and the solid center from which one experiences reality breaks up like a bad radio signal. . . . No core holds things together, providing the lens through which to see the world, to make judgments and comprehend risk. Random moments of time follow one another. Sights, sounds, thoughts, and feelings don't go together.[53]

She hid this experience from her father, feeling that this was a secret that she had to keep.

Saks notes that sometimes her experiences of psychosis would be auditory but other times they would be more like intrusive thoughts. Often they would be negative: *"You are a piece of shit. You don't deserve to be around people. You are nothing. Other people will see this. They will hate you. They will hate you and they will want to hurt you. They can hurt you. They are powerful. You are weak. You are nothing."*[54]

Sometimes these thoughts were commands, such as instructions to hurt herself. "It never occurred to me that disobedience was an option,"[55] she writes, and so she would obey the commands to burn herself with cigarettes, lighters, and heaters.

One of the most notable features of the book is the relationship Saks has with her therapist, Mrs. Jones, a psychoanalyst. Although there is a basic consensus that, for a given mental illness, the best approach is medication *and* therapy, in practice psychiatrists increasingly focus solely on pharmacologic interventions. Therapy is typically performed by other disciplines (e.g., psychologists, social workers, licensed counselors), because this usually costs less and is more available to patients. So, this is why Jamison, Saks, and others spend so much time on making the case for therapy. Yet, among those who advocate for therapy, Saks is nevertheless unusual for her promotion of psychoanalysis, which, due to its not being evidenced based, has fallen out of favor.

Saks includes a copious amount of material from her sessions with Mrs. Jones, including an analysis of her dreams. In one session, Saks recounts this single-sentence dream: "I was making golf balls out of fetuses."[56] Remarkably, Mrs. Jones interprets the dream as follows:

> You want to kill babies, you see, and then make a game out of it. You are jealous of the other babies. Jealous of your brothers, jealous of my other patients. You want to kill them. And then you want to turn them into a little ball so you can smack them again. You want your mother and me to love only you.[57]

From a psychoanalytic point of view, the key to interpreting dreams is that they are wish fulfillments.[58] When the wishes are unacceptable to the dreamer (often because they are sexual or aggressive in nature), the mind disguises the wishes by employing various techniques such as displacement, projection, reversals, condensation, and symbolization. Mrs. Jones's interpretation focused on what she interpreted as disguised aggression (fetuses represent a desire to kill babies) as a result of jealousy, rooted in a desire to have all important people in one's life (one's mother, one's therapist) to oneself.

Reflecting on therapy with Mrs. Jones, Saks noted that Mrs. Jones's words were often *not* comforting but instead were disturbing, though her presence was always calm and nonjudgmental: "No matter what I said to her, no matter how disgusting or horrible, she never recoiled from what I said. To her, my thoughts and feelings were not right or wrong, good or bad; they just were."[59]

It took decades for Saks to accept that she needed to be on medication for the rest of her life. Unlike Jamison, who found positive aspects of her illness, Saks's experience was very different. Indeed, at the end of the book Saks writes in answer to the question: "If there were a pill that would instantly cure me, would I take it?"[60] She gives an unambiguous "Yes" and goes on to say, "Mania in manic depression has been described as a sometimes pleasurable high that brings with it feelings of omnipotence. But that's not the experience of schizophrenia, at least not for me. My psychosis is a waking nightmare."[61] Still, she does not regret being alive. She is grateful for her life and counts it as good fortune for "having found my life."[62] She notes that she has not "recovered" from her mental illness but that she has led a full and rich life, which is what she wants for others with schizophrenia.

Perhaps the most significant and focused issue of advocacy in *The Center Cannot Hold* is the use of mechanical restraints. Saks experienced psychiatric hospitalizations in both the United Kingdom and the United States, and while her experience in the United Kingdom was basically positive, she was traumatized in the United States because of the use of restraints and forced treatment.

Because of her law background, she later wrote an important law article arguing against mechanical restraints in favor of patient autonomy.[63] Today, due to a culture shift, the use of mechanical restraints is much more infrequent than in previous decades. However, the use of chemical restraints is common in inpatient psychiatric hospitals, whereas mechanical restraints are more liberally used in medical settings (such as the emergency department). Saks also makes the case that psychiatric patients should be able to refuse medications on the grounds that, if a person is ever going to be compliant with treatment, they need to have a say.

5.2 Clinical Information

The *DSM-5-TR* lists five key features that define psychotic disorders:

1. Delusions (fixed false beliefs)
2. Hallucinations (false perception-like experiences)
3. Disorganized thinking (e.g., incoherent speech)
4. Grossly disorganized or abnormal motor behavior
5. Negative symptoms (e.g., diminished emotional expression)[64]

To make the diagnosis of schizophrenia, two or more of these five psychotic features must be present for a one-month period, with at least one of the features being delusions, hallucinations, or disorganized speech. There must be a disturbance in social functioning (e.g., work) or self-care. There must be some signs of this disturbance for at least six months, unless successfully treated. And, as with other psychiatric diagnoses, other disorders (especially bipolar disorder with psychotic features) must be ruled out; there must not be another better medical diagnosis; and this disturbance cannot be attributed to substance use or medication. Finally, if there is a history of a communication disorder or autism spectrum disorder, the diagnosis of schizophrenia can only be made if delusions or hallucinations are present.[65]

It could be that what is called schizophrenia today will have a different nomenclature tomorrow. Perhaps there are schizophrenias (thus the term "schizophrenia *spectrum* disorders"),[66] which might be why it was so difficult for Saks to receive a diagnosis. She clearly exhibited many, if not all, of the criteria noted by the *DSM-5-TR*.

What this pathography does especially well is demonstrate Saks's delusions and incoherent speech. Although Jamison experienced delusions and hallucinations, which Saks also experienced, Saks displayed the common symptom of speaking in so-called word salads. She writes: "The technical term for what I was doing (where one says words that sound similar but have no real connection with one another) is 'word salad' – although in my case, 'fruit salad' might have been more apropos."[67] As an example, she offers this: "My name is Elyn. They used to call me 'Elyn, Elyn, watermelon.' At school. Where I used to go. Where I am now and having trouble."[68]

Her therapist (a psychiatry intern) asks: What kind of trouble? She responds:

> There's trouble. Right here in River City. Home of the New Haveners. Where there is no haven, new or old. I'm just looking for a haven. Can you give me a haven? Aren't you too young? Why are you crying? I cry because the voices are at the end of time. Time is too old. I've killed lots of people.[69]

Saks's story can be used to better understand the clinical criterion that if a symptom can be explained by another medical condition, that diagnosis should be considered before making a psychiatric one or lumping the symptom in with an existing psychiatric diagnosis. When persons with mental illness have other medical problems, these medical problems are sometimes routinely dismissed because of the psychiatric diagnosis, with serious consequences. For example, after experiencing severe headaches, Saks went to the emergency department. However, when it was discovered that she had a psychiatric history, her symptoms were assumed to be the result of her mental illness. In fact, she was having a subarachnoid hemorrhage. She was just thirty-two years old.[70] She was almost sent home, but the hemorrhage was detected when an attending physician asked "if it hurt when my legs were raised and I tried to touch my toes with my fingers at the same time."[71] It did. A spinal tap was ordered and the brain bleed was revealed. This episode dramatically brings to light an otherwise mundane specification in the *DSM*.

6 Addiction

6.1 Beautiful Boy

Beautiful Boy and *Tweak* are a remarkable pair of books written by a father and his son about the son's addiction. *Beautiful Boy* by David Sheff portrays the father's perspective and *Tweak* by Nic Sheff offers his son's. Although both books are insightful in their own right, reading them together is a powerful exercise in point of view.

The primary focus of *Beautiful Boy* is on Nic. As a father, David wants to understand his son's addiction to methamphetamines, how it happened and what can be done to save his son. The book is full of painful introspection, especially as David wonders what role his divorce and other actions played in his son's life: "I am aghast at so much of what I did and, equally, what I did not do. .... I often feel as though I completely failed my son."[72] The book chronicles so many of the starts and stops of addiction, the hoping and the lying. Strikingly, David comes to the realization that "I became addicted to my son's addiction" and that, although a devastating realization, "our children live or die with or without us."[73] Nevertheless, David wishes that he would have intervened in his son's life earlier, without full confidence that it would have made a difference.

David takes up the issue of divorce early in the book, noting that he and Vicki (Nic's mother) divorced before Nic was five years old. Vicki moved to Los Angeles, while David stayed in San Francisco. A judge ordered that Nic would stay with his father during the school year but spend the summers with his mother. So, at the age of five Nic was flying alone. And he came to resent his summers in Los Angeles because his friends were in San Francisco. When Nic turned nine, David married Karen. David and Karen have two children together, and both adore Nic.

David eventually concludes that Nic's addiction cannot be attributed to the divorce but that the divorce intimately contributed to Nic's personality and character. David notes that, although divorce is difficult for all children, Nic should not have been forced to commute between two cities, adding: "he has more frequent-flyer miles than most adults."[74]

In high school, Nic won an essay contest, writing about his experience of the divorce, which was published in *Newsweek*. Quoting Nic, David writes:

> Maybe there should be an addition to the marriage vows. .... Do you promise to love and to hold, for richer and for poorer, in sickness and in health, as long as you both shall live? And if you have children and wind up divorced, do you promise to stay within the same geographic area as your kids? Actually, since people so often break those vows, maybe it should be a law: If you have children, you must stay near them. Or how about some common sense: If you move away from your children, you have to do the traveling to see them.[75]

Although David is highly self-critical regarding the divorce, Nic's rebuke seems directed at his mother for moving.

The book is notable for the research that David did. So much of it is interesting and compelling. He found, for example, that drugs from the 1960s were, in fact, significantly less potent than today, as is often said, because psychedelics now are routinely laced with meth. Also, in the 1960s and 1970s it was assumed that marijuana was basically safe, but today a body of research is emerging that it is not as harmless as assumed, some studies pointing to a link between early marijuana use and the onset of serious mental illness such as schizophrenia.[76]

David writes about his own drug use, which he describes as excessive at times.[77] David and Nic did smoke pot together, which, in retrospect, seems questionable at best. As a parent, David writes about the difficulty in knowing what to do: "Friends and family offer contradictory advice: Kick him out, don't let him out of your sight. I think: Kick him out? What chance will he have then? Don't let him out of my sight? *You* try corralling a seventeen-year-old on drugs."[78] If dealing with a teenager is hard enough, reasoning with a teenager on meth is exponentially more problematic because, for meth addicts to recover in terms of brain function, David found that it takes about two years of sobriety.[79]

David vacillates on whether to blame Nic for his relapses. David expressed surprise to learn that, as a parent, your hopes – or rationalizations – for your child are almost infinitely malleable: "He's just experimenting. Going through a stage. It's only marijuana. He gets high only on weekends. At least he's not using hard drugs. At least it's not heroin. He would never resort to needles. At least he's alive."[80] Struggling with his own guilt, shame, and helplessness, David found it helpful to view addiction as a disease. He points out that if we as a society really believed addiction to be a disease, we would not leave these children suffering on the streets. If these kids had cancer, there would be all kinds of fundraisers and political support; they would not be abandoned. Based on the uncertainties he experienced as the parent of an addicted son, at the end of the book, David offers some policy recommendations regarding how to help persons with addiction.

6.2 Tweak

In reading *Tweak* after *Beautiful Boy*, perhaps the most conspicuous feature is the relative absence of David in Nic's telling of the story. This is reflected in the book's dedication, to two women in Nic's life (neither are family members): "You are the two people I respect and admire most in the world."[81] This act underscores that the story told in this book has a very different perspective than *Beautiful Boy*.

Still, Nic acknowledges that "Every time I've gotten sober in the past my dad has reemerged as one of my closest friends."[82] Also, regarding the divorce of his parents and his childhood, he concedes that he does not blame his father for anything that transpired and that he appreciates the way he was raised. On reflection, Nic does indicate that he felt abandoned by his mother when she moved and also by his father when he remarried: "My dad was trying so hard to leave his old life behind, and I can see now that I felt like it was a rejection of me. I felt like I was a mistake and that my dad wanted to correct me along with everything else."[83]

The book begins with Nic being sober for eighteen months, feeling as though he had finally gotten control of his life. He recalls that, when he tried meth for the first time, "[t]here was a feeling like – my God, this is what I have been missing my entire life. It completed me. I felt whole for the first time."[84] He adds: "I guess I've pretty much spent the last four years chasing that first high. I wanted desperately to feel that wholeness again."[85] But Nic describes, bluntly, the effects of his addiction on his life: "I dropped out of college twice, my parents kicked me out, and, basically, my life unraveled. I broke into their house – I would steal checks from my father and write them out to myself to pay for my habit. When I had a job at a coffee shop, I stole hundreds of dollars from the register."[86] He reflects that, although he did not want to stop using, he also recognized that these actions were against his moral code.

At one point when Nic was living in New York City, he would prostitute himself to men to make money. He recalls one promiscuous night during which he overdosed and ended up in the emergency department: "I'd been up for a couple of days doing coke and crystal and drinking. . . . I ended up back at my apartment in the middle of this orgy of guys. Vaguely I remember someone eating out my ass, while my dick refused to get hard. Then I gave up and let whoever wanted to fuck me, fuck me."[87]

After these incidences, he felt deep shame, and would turn to using drugs again both to experience pleasure and to numb his emotional pain. Because of its unflinching openness, there is a rawness to Nic's pathography that is not present in David's.

Outward appearance and social status are major themes in Nic's pathography. This may be linked to the fact that both his parents maintained connections with celebrities. Nic writes: "There is something about outward appearances that has always been important to me. I always thought I was so ugly."[88] He adds: "I mean, I really did. I remember being in L.A. at my mom's house as a little kid and just staring into the mirror for hours. It was, like, if I looked long enough, maybe I'd finally be handsome. It never worked. I just got uglier and uglier."[89] It is not surprising, therefore, that David titled his book *Beautiful Boy*, trying to convince his son that he is, in fact, beautiful.

Toward the end of the book, Nic reconnects with a former lover, Zelda, who, according to Nic, is somewhat of a celebrity. The couple moves in together, and even talks about marriage. She draws Nic into an elite social scene filled with drugs and partying. Catastrophe follows and Nic's life implodes again.

Rehab provided Nic the insight that life with Zelda would never bring happiness; and in group therapy, he came to the realization of a possible connection between his longing for Zelda and his longing as a child for his mother – both were unavailable women whom Nic wanted to rescue. Once sober, and this time wanting to build a new life, he moved away from the influences of California and New York, settling down in Savannah, Georgia.

In his memoir, Zelda's importance cannot be overstated. She is the narrative engine that drives the story. If it were not for her, Nic may not have relapsed, and, without working through his relationship with Zelda, it is possible that he would not have recovered. Although Zelda is mentioned in *Beautiful Boy*, she is absolutely central in *Tweak*.

In an afterword, Nic discloses that he had a minor relapse (with pills), but notes that he was able to avoid falling into his previous cycle. If it is true that addiction is "a disease of amnesia,"[90] Nic finally learned enough from his previous descents into the depths about how to climb to recovery.

An important dynamic, and a key element to Nic's recovery that is not meaningfully explored in the book is the fact that, in addition to addiction, he was also being treated for bipolar illness. Often, addiction is a complicating factor when treating patients with other forms of mental illness, such as, in Nic's case, bipolar disorder. Both need to be treated, but it is not uncommon for patients to only be treated for one, thus greatly lessening the chances for progress.

Another topic that Nic insightfully raises in the afterword is the ethics of telling someone else's story. Although the story that he told was his own, it also involved other people. He suggests that some people in the book, such as Zelda, are easily identifiable and that by sharing her story without permission, he no doubt added to her suffering. The ethics of storytelling are relevant in all pathographies, but they are often not considered, and it is noteworthy that Nic does, if only in retrospect.

6.3 Clinical Information

The *DSM-5-TR* has a section on substance-related and addictive disorders with ten different classes of drugs, from tobacco and caffeine to alcohol and cocaine. It notes that often these drugs are not completely distinct, and also that all drugs, when taken in excess, activate reward systems in the brain, making it difficult to stop.

A substance use disorder is "a cluster of cognitive, behavioral, and physiological symptoms indicating that the individual continues using the substance despite significant substance-related problems."[91] It offers eleven criteria to help identify the disorder. All of these criteria must be related to use of the substance:

1. Uses more of the substance than intended
2. Unsuccessful in attempts to reduce use
3. Spends a great deal of time on the substance

4. Experiences strong craving
5. Fails to fulfill personal, social, and occupational roles
6. Interpersonal problems
7. Activities are relinquished
8. Enters hazardous situations
9. Physical and psychological harm occurs
10. Develops tolerance
11. Experiences withdrawal[92]

The *DSM-5-TR* also distinguishes according to severity: mild (two to three symptoms), moderate (four to five symptoms), and severe (six or more symptoms).

It is clear that Nic fits the clinical criteria for substance use disorder; but the clinical criterion that he is unsuccessful in reducing use is especially noteworthy. Although this can be commonly applied to everyone struggling with addiction, what Nic's story adds is a particular existential dimension. At one point, Nic tells his friend, Gack, who also is a meth user, that he is thinking about getting clean. Gack balks and says: "What is life for, if not for living?" Nic responds: "Is this living?" And Gack says, "We're so free."[93] He adds: "You only get to live this life once. I'd rather be blissed out for a short time than fucking bored and miserable till I'm like ninety or something."[94]

What is telling about this conversation is that it represents an ideological concept of happiness. For Nic, and perhaps others struggling with addiction, not only is there the difficulty of overcoming the physiological aspects of addiction (e.g., withdrawal), but also there is a system of thinking to work through as well: If the point of life is to experience as much pleasure as possible, then why not do meth? A prescription cannot answer this question.

7 Borderline Personality Disorder

7.1 Girl, Interrupted

Girl, Interrupted by Susanna Kaysen is also a classic in the field of pathography. With help from a lawyer, Kaysen obtained copies of her medical records, which she had reproduced and printed in her book (setting the stage for a number of other pathographies to employ the same strategy[95]). The book focuses on her stay at McLean Hospital, Harvard's private psychiatric facility in Belmont, Massachusetts.

Kaysen opens her memoir by addressing the question of how one gets admitted to a psychiatric hospital, underscoring the fact that people want assurance that they will not end up there. But Kaysen does not offer this assurance. She writes: "It's easy," adding that "most people pass over incrementally."[96] Kaysen checked herself into the hospital because, as she put it, she was having problems with patterns. Although not hallucinating, ordinary items, like rugs, seemed to contain other things inside of them and reality became so dense that her efforts to cope were exhausting. It became difficult to focus on faces and she had trouble connecting with people. Kaysen adds that that time itself seemed to be different for her, especially when in the hospital: "It may run in circles, flow backward, skip about from now to then."[97] Throughout much of the book, Kaysen is concerned with time, in part as a way to find out for herself whether she is a credible narrator.

When Kaysen was admitted to McLean in 1967, it was before the process of de-institutionalization in the United States and long stays in psychiatric hospitals were routine. It was a common trope in books and movies that patients in these hospitals were compared to prisoners. This pathography follows in that angry spirit, with an emphasis on gender; it is a book of protest.

Kaysen indicates that, as a part of her diagnosis, her psychiatrists cited "compulsive promiscuity."[98] She admits flirting and acting inappropriately with a teacher in high school.[99] She also describes a system of "five-minute checks," during which nurses would come into their rooms if they had male visitors, going on to describe what can – and cannot – be done sexually in five minutes. And Kaysen mentions a brief interaction with James Watson, who, in 1962 along with Francis Crick and Maurice Wilkins, won the Nobel Prize for their discovery of the molecular structure of DNA. At the time of the reported encounter, Watson would have been approaching the age of forty and not yet married; Kaysen was eighteen. According to Kaysen, in this unexpected visit Watson asked her to leave the hospital and run away with him to England but she declined, saying, "I think I've got to stay here."[100] It is a little unclear what to make of the encounter, but, as reviewer Alan Stone has noted, if true, this speaks to Watson's poor judgment and Kaysen's "mini-skirted magnetism."[101]

In writing *Girl, Interrupted*, it was not Kaysen's intention to write a traditional pathography. Reflecting decades later on the success of the book, she notes in an interview with Tara Merrigan that she wanted to write as though she were an anthropologist doing an ethnography from the inside of a psychiatric hospital. Merrigan writes: "She told me that the last thing she was trying to do was write about her own life."[102] Kaysen adds: "I don't write about my family really. I don't write that much about my internal state. It's not about me."[103] Instead, she wrote about other patients, the residents, the doctors, and the nurses.

She includes the stories of a number of the other women in the hospital. About their illnesses, she sums it up succinctly: "Cynthia was depressive; Polly and Georgina were schizophrenic; I had a character disorder. Sometimes they called it a personality disorder. When I got my diagnosis it didn't sound serious, but after a while it sounded more ominous than other people's."[104] She adds:

> If my diagnosis had been bipolar illness, for instance, the reaction to me and to this story would be slightly different. That's a chemical problem, you'd say to yourself, manic-depression, Lithium, all that. I would be blameless, somehow. And what about schizophrenia – that would send a chill up your spine. After all, that's real insanity. People don't "recover" from schizophrenia. You'd have to wonder how much of what I am telling you is true and how much imagined.[105]

It is interesting to see how writers of pathographies self-assess in terms of their mental illness as compared to others. Kaysen makes note of the fact when others clearly have it worse than she does. About Polly, who lit her face on fire and was deformed, she writes: "Who would kiss a person like that, a person with no skin?"[106] She adds: "We might get out [of the hospital] sometime, but she was locked up forever in that body."[107]

At McLean, many of the young women had attempted suicide, including Kaysen herself, two years before her psychiatric hospitalization. Kaysen has some poignant insights to add: "Suicide is a form of murder – premeditated murder."[108] Like any successful murder, Kaysen says that it takes time, thought, motive, detachment, and organization. In her own case, she describes her motive as weak and so she did not complete her suicide. But she adds: "It was only part of myself that I wanted to kill: the part that wanted to kill herself, that dragged me into the suicide debate and made every window, kitchen implement, and subway station a rehearsal for tragedy. I didn't figure this out, though, until after I'd swallowed the fifty aspirin."[109]

It was this suicide attempt that justified diagnosing a mental illness. Her psychiatrists chose borderline personality disorder because she had problems with identity and direction in life. As noted, her promiscuity was a factor – but how do we know promiscuity, clinically, when we see it? She was told that she cannot make a life out of boyfriends and literature, to which she wondered: Why not? She did not feel as though her self-image was unstable; she felt that the image of her *from the perspective of others* was unstable. She knew that society was sexist, and she resented being forced to comply with patriarchal norms, and thus resisted. When confronted with the *DSM*, she acknowledged that the description of borderline personality disorder was "a fairly accurate picture of me at eighteen," but that this wasn't "profound."[110]

In terms of describing what borderline personality disorder might be like from the patient's point of view, this passage in the book comes the closest to doing so:

My ambition was to negate. ... When I was supposed to be awake, I was asleep; when I was supposed to speak, I was silent; when a pleasure offered itself to me, I avoided it. My hunger, my thirst, my loneliness and boredom and fear were all weapons aimed at my enemy, the world. ... All my integrity seemed to lie in saying No.[111]

Toward the end of the book, she reflects on the title of the book, a reference to Johannes Vermeer's painting *Girl Interrupted at Her Music*, which she had seen as part of the Frick collection in New York. She writes: "Interrupted at her music: as my life had been, interrupted in the music of being seventeen, as her life had been, snatched and fixed on canvas."[112] She concludes the book by reflecting on light: "We wish the sun could make us young and beautiful ... [and] we wish everyone we knew could be brightened simply by our looking at them. ... The girl at her music sits in another sort of light, the fitful, overcast light of life, by which we see ourselves and others only imperfectly, and seldom."[113]

7.2 Clinical Information

The *DSM-5-TR* defines borderline personality disorder as consisting of at least five of the following characteristics:

1. Frantic efforts to avoid abandonment
2. Unstable interpersonal relationships
3. Identity disturbance
4. Impulsivity
5. Suicidal or self-harming behavior or threats of such behavior
6. Affective instability
7. Feelings of emptiness
8. Inappropriate anger
9. Paranoid ideation or dissociative symptoms[114]

For decades this diagnosis has been gendered. The *DSM-5*, for example, states that borderline personality disorder is predominately (75 percent) diagnosed in females,[115] but the *DSM-5-TR* drops this statistic and instead has this statement: "While borderline personality disorder is more common among women than men in clinical samples, community samples demonstrate no difference between men and women."[116]

In the discussion of Saks, the importance of considering medical diagnoses when making a psychiatric diagnosis was noted. This is also true of borderline personality disorder, as well as all mental disorders. But here it should be underscored that the *DSM-5-TR* indicates that borderline personality disorder should not be confused with identity problems, especially those during adolescence, which are normal. Though she did not use this term, Kaysen's time in the psychiatric hospital could be thought of what Erik Erikson called a psychosocial moratorium: a break away from obligations and decisions young adults sometimes need as they begin to form their identity.[117] As Kaysen puts it: "For many of us, the hospital was as much a refuge as it was a prison. Though we were cut off from the world and all the trouble we enjoyed stirring up out there, we were also cut off from the demands and expectations that had driven us crazy."[118] It could be that Kaysen suffered from borderline personality disorder, or it could be that she just needed time. In the book and in subsequent interviews, the question remains open.

8 Conduct Disorder

8.1 A Mother's Reckoning

In *A Mother's Reckoning*, Sue Klebold writes about the shooting at Columbine High School on April 20, 1999, carried out by Eric Harris and her son Dylan Klebold. Friends and classmates, Eric and Dylan killed twelve students and a teacher, wounding twenty-four others before killing themselves. Since the University of Texas tower shooting on August 1, 1966, this was the first major school shooting in the United States. Although there were many others between these events, it was the first to be covered by the modern media and subsequently became a well-known public tragedy.

The book is a painful, introspective search of a mother trying to find out what went wrong with her son: "Sixteen years have passed since that terrible day, and I have dedicated them to understanding what is still incomprehensible to me – how a promising boy's life could have escalated into such a disaster, and on my watch."[119] Sue adds that she and her husband, Tom, were loving and engaged parents, that their lives were ordinary, and that Dylan was an affectionate child. When did things go off track, and why?

As the events unfolded on April 20, 1999, Sue and Tom went from at first receiving no information from the police to being overwhelmed by the media coverage. Sue writes that, initially, she could not accept that Dylan had actually taken part, then thinking that he was tricked in some way, that it was a prank gone wrong, or that he was coerced. After Dylan's death, Sue and Tom hoped that the autopsy would reveal that Dylan had been using drugs, which would then explain his behavior. Eventually she had to give up all of these rationalizations. Sue remembers that in her grief she suffered pain in her chest so acute that she believed she had literal confirmation of what it meant to have a broken heart.

Sue regrets that Dylan did not leave a suicide note because she will never know his motive for committing the massacre. In the beginning she points out that the mass of media misinformation quickly became the official narrative, and it provided a reason for her to hold onto false beliefs: "If they'd gotten this fact wrong, or that one, then perhaps all of it was false."[120]

Sue sees her book as a way to set the record straight. Dylan was not an outcast; he had good and close friends. She pushed back against the image of Dylan as a "swastika-wearing" hater, and she pointed out that observing Passover Seder was part of family tradition. The media tried to paint Dylan as "spoiled" because he drove a BMW, but she noted that they bought the car for $400.

A major factor in Sue's grieving process involved the loss of identity – Dylan's identity, her identity, and the identity of the family unit. The countless accusations aimed at them as parents were wide ranging. Some called them too lenient and others too restrictive. Some felt that they should have exposed Dylan to guns to normalize his use of firearms. Others suspected that Dylan was abused or deprived of affection. She adds: "People blamed video games, movies, music, bullying, access to guns, unarmed teachers, the absence of prayer in schools, secular humanism, psychiatric medication. Mostly, though, they blamed us. To me, that made sense. . . . I would have blamed us too."[121] Upon reflection, though, Sue writes:

> The disquieting reality is that behind this heinous atrocity was an easygoing, shy, likeable young man who came from a "good home." Tom and I were hands-on parents who limited the intake of television and sugary cereals. We monitored what movies our boys could see, and put them to bed with stories and prayers and hugs. . . . Dylan was the classic good kid.[122]

Still, there were some concerning earlier episodes, such as when Dylan and Eric broke into a van and were caught by the police, or when his parents discovered marijuana in his room. Dylan also got in trouble at school for breaking into lockers, and he had some traffic tickets. There was a disturbing paper that he turned in for one of his classes, in which a man dressed in black kills the popular kids at school.[123]

Sue recalls that when Dylan was in ninth grade, he failed to make the baseball team, which was a great loss for him. It was at this time that he switched his attention from sports to computers. Sue and Tom did not monitor Dylan's computer and internet activity and in retrospect she comments: "This seems shockingly naive now, but it was a different time – and anyway, I would not have known how to check his browser history or usage in those days; I had only just begun using the internet myself."[124]

It was confirmed that Dylan played an active role in planning the massacre and in buying guns; he was not merely a passive participant. As she tried to grapple with the reality of her son's actions, Sue felt that "[i]t was easier for me to believe he had been crazy – or even evil – than to pretend anything he'd experienced could justify what he'd done."[125] At times she wondered if he were demon-possessed.

After his death, to her surprise, Sue found a pack of cigarettes in his room. She was forced to concede that not only was Dylan capable of hiding things from her, but also, because of their recent conversation about the dangers of smoking, deliberately lying. Additionally, she discovered a bottle of St. John's-wort, a natural anti-depressant: "Here was bald, incontrovertible evidence that Dylan had been depressed enough to try to alleviate those feelings through medication. The expiration date on the bottle indicated he had it a long time."[126] In the end, this was a partial explanation that she found somewhat helpful in that Dylan's destructive behavior was rooted in his unrecognized and untreated depression. For this reason, the central message of her book, like *Beautiful Boy*, is one of advocacy: there should be more active mental health screening in schools.

For Sue, depression also explained Dylan's connection with Eric, whom Sue characterized as an evil sociopath, responsible for egging him on. Thomas Joiner, a psychologist who reviewed the journals of Eric and Dylan, concluded: "Dylan appears to have 'needed' Eric's homicidal plan in order to be able to do what he most wanted to do: die by suicide."[127] He adds: "Dylan's writing is jumbled, disorganized, and full of tangled syntax and misused words. Eric's *thoughts* are disturbing; Dylan's thought *process* is disturbed. The difference is in what Eric thinks and how Dylan thinks."[128]

As a teenager, Eric was referred to a psychiatrist for his angry outbursts and his behavioral issues, but it is unclear if he received a diagnosis of conduct disorder.[129] After the shooting, the FBI ascertained that the original plan for the shooting was Eric's, and that Eric tried to recruit other boys to join him, but they declined. Sue notes that some psychologists concluded that "Eric relied on Dylan's slow-burning, depressive anger to fuel and feed his sadism, while Dylan used Eric's destructive impulses to jolt him out of his passivity."[130]

In any case, Sue reaches the conclusion that "[e]very belief I had created in order to survive had been shredded,"[131] as it became clear that Eric and Dylan were trying to blow up the school. When she watched the so-called basement tapes (recordings that Eric and Dylan made prior to their deaths), she observed that: "Neither one of them acknowledges a connection between the actions they are planning and the pain they will cause the people who love them."[132] She adds: "In another recording, they go so far as to announce that their parents and friends hold no responsibility for what is about to happen, as if tidying up this minor detail will make everything fine for their families when it's all over."[133]

Dylan went to prom three days before the shooting. When he returned home, he displayed a full flask of alcohol, thus demonstrating to his parents that they could trust him not to drink. Sue writes: "In retrospect, I sometimes think that engaging me in that conversation about the flask was among the cruelest tricks Dylan ever played on me. Was he consciously manipulating me into trusting him, even as he was planning a massacre? Was he mocking me?"[134] She adds: "If he was preparing to die within a few days, why was it necessary to establish my trust in him? Did he need reassurance, or was he trying to prevent me from searching his room?"[135]

Looking back, she regrets not listening to Dylan enough, and she wishes that she had spent time with him just acknowledging his feelings. When reading his journal after his death, Sue discovered that Dylan had entertained suicidal ideation for at least two years prior to the event and his entries were filled with what may be taken as suicide notes. The journal revealed that he was painfully infatuated with a girl with whom he had no connection, and also that he was involved in cutting himself. She has deep regrets that she did not read his journals sooner, recognizing the moral ambiguity of such action: "When we search our children's rooms or read their journals, we risk that they will feel betrayed. However, they may be hiding problems they cannot manage by themselves."[136]

8.2 Clinical Information

The *DSM-5-TR* states that disruptive, impulse control, and conduct disorders involve problems with emotional regulation and self-control, adding that while other disorders have these characteristics, what makes these distinctive is that they involve violations of the rights of others or conflicts with social norms and authority figures.[137] With regard to conduct disorder, there is a consistent pattern of this kind of behavior with at least three of the following criteria for twelve months and at least one present during the last six months:

1. Bullying
2. Fighting
3. Using a weapon
4. Being physically cruel to people
5. Being physically cruel to animals
6. Confrontationally stealing (e.g., mugging)
7. Sexual assault or rape
8. Fire setting with intent to damage property
9. Destruction of someone else's property (excluding fire setting)
10. Breaking and entering
11. Lies

12. Theft and forgery (i.e., nonphysical stealing without breaking and entering)
13. Stays out at night against the wishes of parents (prior to age thirteen)
14. Runs away from home (at least twice or once for a long period)
15. Truancy from school (prior to age thirteen)[138]

The *DSM-5-TR* notes that this behavior causes an impairment in social functioning. Also, if a person is over the age of eighteen but does not meet the criteria for antisocial personality disorder, they may be given this diagnosis.[139]

The *DSM-5-TR* includes subtypes – childhood onset, adolescent onset, or unspecified – along with degree of severity (mild, moderate, or severe), as well as an additional specifier of limited prosocial emotions (i.e., lack of remorse or empathy, a shallow affect, or being unconcerned about performance). The *DSM-5* suggests that this disorder appears to be more prevalent in males than females, and, when present in females, the manifestation of aggression often is relational in nature. While cultural context should be considered with all forms of mental illness, the *DSM-5* also emphasizes that conduct disorder may be inappropriately applied in settings of war or high crime.[140] However, the *DSM-5-TR* drops the suggestion that this disorder may be more prevalent in boys and men, instead focusing on how the disorder can manifest differently in girls and women.[141] The *DSM-5-TR* retains the point about culture.

In a sense, it seems as though any child involved with a mass shooting would, by default, be diagnosed with conduct disorder. Dylan used a weapon, was physically cruel to people, destroyed property, and lied (four of the criteria, when only three are needed). Yet, if his mother's account is accurate, the diagnosis of conduct disorder does not seem to fit because he was, for the most part, a "good kid." According to Sue, it would seem that Eric – and *not* Dylan – would fit the diagnosis of conduct disorder. But is Sue's perspective reliable?

It is important to make clear here that, unlike the other sections in this Element (where a psychiatric diagnosis was given by a professional), as far as I have been able to discern, no psychiatrist officially diagnosed either Dylan or Eric with conduct disorder. When an expert did weigh in on a diagnosis for Dylan, Sue notes that Peter Langman (an expert on school shooters) felt that Dylan may have suffered from avoidant personality disorder as a boy and later progressed to schizotypal personality disorder as a teenager.[142]

9 Antisocial Personality Disorder

9.1 My Friend Dahmer

Like the shooting at Columbine High School, the serial killings of Jeffrey Dahmer gained international attention. The nature of the murders – especially because Dahmer claimed to have cannibalized some of his victims, plus the deviant sexual nature of the crimes – contributed to Dahmer's infamy. In the end, Dahmer admitted to raping and murdering seventeen boys and men in Ohio and Wisconsin. There is some speculation that there may have been more.

Dahmer continues to have a profound cultural impact. He is routinely mentioned in the media,[143] TV shows and movies have been made about him,[144] he features as the main character in a fictional novel,[145] and he has even inspired musical compositions. A pastor wrote about his experience of visiting with Dahmer in prison, leading up to Dahmer's conversion and baptism.[146] He is, in short, one of the most well-known of all serial killers.

Derf Backderf, who went to high school with Dahmer, wrote a graphic novel titled, *My Friend Dahmer*.[147] It focuses on his youth, and it provides material that suggests a diagnosis of conduct disorder. His behavior as an adult is so well-known that the diagnosis of antisocial personality disorder seems obvious. George Palermo, one of the court-appointed forensic psychiatrists involved with Dahmer's trial, has affirmed this diagnosis.[148]

Backderf sets out to portray Dahmer as a sympathetic character. Yet, he clearly draws a line where his sympathy ends:

> It's my belief that Dahmer didn't have to wind up a monster, that all those people didn't have to die horribly, if only the adults in his life hadn't been so inexplicably, unforgivably, incomprehensibly clueless and/or indifferent. Once Dahmer kills, however – and I cannot stress this enough – my empathy for him ends. He could have turned himself in after that first murder.[149]

The book begins with Dahmer walking alone down a road where he finds a dead cat. He carries it to a shed behind his house where, using acid stolen from his father's laboratory, he dissolves animals in jars. When Dahmer runs into some other kids from town and they ask why he is playing with dead animals, he explains: "It interests me. What's inside a body."[150] The kids, rather than being intrigued or impressed, call him a freak.

Backderf recalls that he met Dahmer in seventh grade and that Dahmer was "a nobody," someone barely noticed. Bullies who did notice him called him "Dumber" instead of Dahmer. Dahmer's home life was strained. His mother suffered from seizures and appears to have had neurological and/or psychiatric problems. His parents fought bitterly and eventually divorced.

As the years progressed, Dahmer started acting out in school, causing problems for his teachers by behaving like the class clown, throwing fake epileptic seizures, and creating outrageous scenes. His classmates, including Backderf, began to take notice, thinking he was strange but funny. In tenth grade, Backderf created the Dahmer Fan Club. He drew humorous pictures of

Dahmer, such as Dahmer as a bag of groceries or Dahmer as a telephone pole. Still, Backderf writes:

> Dahmer was never asked to join us, even though I drove right past his house on the way to pick up some of the other guys. .... Some instinct warned me off. I was always wary of Dahmer. I was willing to hang out with him at school, but there was no way I was going to forge a closer friendship.[151]

Backderf remembers walking with Dahmer when they saw a classmate slip and fall in front of them, hurting himself badly. Dahmer laughed loudly and cruelly, without a trace of empathy, which struck Backderf as very disturbing. It was moments like these that caused Backderf to maintain a healthy distance from Dahmer.

Backderf writes about his own sexual impulses as a teenage boy, and Dahmer's, too, which Dahmer, knowing that his urges to rape were sick, was loath to disclose. Not having anywhere or anybody to turn to, Dahmer abused alcohol to numb himself, drinking daily at school where, even if an adult did notice, no one seemed to care. Backderf recalls one teacher bragging that he could roll a joint faster than a student. Backderf speculates that if circumstances had been different with the presence of an adult who noticed – and *cared* – Dahmer would have spent his life "doped up on antidepressants and living in his dad's spare room," and this would have been "a sad, lonely life that Dahmer gladly would have accepted over the hellish future that awaited him."[152]

Backderf recalls that everyone in the Dahmer Fan Club had their own moment when they realized Dahmer was "truly scary." His moment occurred when he and Dahmer went to the mall with another friend. On the way, Dahmer disgusted and disturbed him by chugging a complete six pack of beers, one after another. At the mall, they coaxed Dahmer into playing a number of childish pranks, such as knocking over people's drinks while they were dining. Backderf also remembers making plans with the other friend for later that evening, in Dahmer's presence without inviting him. Toward the end of high school, Dahmer was excluded from their group altogether.

Backderf describes his most surreal memory of Dahmer as the time during the school's annual variety show when Backderf did a comedy bit dressed up as Adolf Hitler. After the show, Backderf talked with Dahmer in the hallway: "Me, dressed up as Hitler, chatting with Jeffrey Dahmer! Whenever I think about it, I can only laugh in disbelief."[153]

Shortly before graduation, Dahmer's parents divorced and his father was forced to move out of the house. His mother took David, her other son, with her to move to Wisconsin, leaving Dahmer alone in the house until his father moved back in. It was during this period that he committed his first murder. Later that year, Dahmer left for college but he flunked out of Ohio State University after one quarter.

This is where the novel ends, having covered Dahmer from the age of twelve. It does include the first murder, but does not depict it, thus relieving an anxiety (likely to occur in readers of this pathography) of being subjected to illustrations of the murders.

9.2 Clinical Information

Here is a case report that describes Dahmer's behavior as an adult and assumes the diagnosis of antisocial personality disorder with psychopathic features:

> At age 18, while driving his parents' car, Jeffrey gave a ride to a young man who was walking along the road stripped to the waist. Jeffrey was impressed by his looks, and he invited him to his home for a drink with the hope of having sex with him. When the boy refused his advances and wanted to leave, Jeffrey strangled him and sexually abused him. He later stated that he could not stand the idea of being abandoned and he experienced an irresistible desire to keep the boy with him. He later went on to kill 16 more victims, all adolescents and young men. As his obsession grew, he began saving body parts. He wanted to remember the appearance of his victims, and he took pictures of the corpses. They belonged to him. He exercised total control over his victims to the point that he attempted to make zombies out of some of them: He gave them alcohol in which sleep-inducing drugs were dissolved, and when they were half-asleep, he drilled holes in their skulls and injected muriatic acid into them to liquefy the brain matter, but when his experiment failed, he murdered them. The skulls of the six victims on whom he had perpetrated the horrendous act were found in his apartment at the time of his apprehension.[154]

The key feature of antisocial personality disorder is that it exhibits "a pervasive pattern of disregard for, and violation of, the rights of others."[155] It manifests with at least three of the following characteristics:

1. Unlawful behavior
2. Deceitfulness
3. Impulsiveness
4. Aggressiveness
5. Disregard for safety
6. Irresponsibly (e.g., in work or financial matters)
7. Lack of remorse[156]

Also, persons must be over the age of eighteen. If younger, conduct disorder should be considered. If they have been diagnosed with conduct disorder as a child, this also is a diagnostic criterion for antisocial personality disorder as an adult. The *DSM-5-TR* adds that antisocial behavior must not occur only when experiencing schizophrenia or bipolar disorder.[157]

According to the *DSM-5-TR* "lack of empathy, inflated self-appraisal, and superficial charm are features that have been commonly included in traditional conceptions of psychopathy that may be particularly distinguishing of the disorder and more predictive of recidivism in prison or forensic settings."[158] It adds that, while this disorder does appear to be more prevalent in urban areas among those with low socioeconomic status, there is ambiguity here because, culturally speaking, these behaviors may be "a protective survival strategy."[159] It is diagnosed more often in men, but it may be underdiagnosed in women.

It is important to notice that not all criminal behavior indicates a diagnosis of antisocial personality disorder, but only when these "traits are inflexible, maladaptive, and persistent and cause significant functional impairment or subjective distress."[160] With perhaps the exception of impulsiveness and irresponsibility, Dahmer exhibited all of the criteria as a serial killer. As a rule, he was methodical and careful, until his alcoholism got out of control, which led to his arrest.

One feature of deceitfulness that does not come across clearly in the *DSM-5-TR* (but does in *My Friend Dahmer*) is just how compelling these persons can be, a feature often missing in articles and case reports. Backderf recalls a high school trip where he, Dahmer, and others went to Washington, DC, to learn about the federal government. During the trip, Dahmer did not drink and his behavior was not unlike a normal teenager. The group joked about calling the Vice President's Office, but Dahmer actually did it. Dahmer was so charming on the phone that, amazingly, he and others were invited into Vice President Walter Mondale's office! (Seeing this drawing, too, is much more forceful than reading about this occurrence, demonstrating the power of graphic medicine.) Although this was a remarkably positive experience for all of them, in most other instances in his life it seems that Dahmer used his charm to harm victims or to lie to legal authorities, clinical personnel, or family members.

10 Autism Spectrum Disorder

10.1 The Reason I Jump

Naoki Higashida's *The Reason I Jump* is a remarkable book, written by a Japanese thirteen-year-old boy whose autism prevents him from normal verbal communication. He wrote his pathography by means of a computer with help from an aide. Higashida begins by noting that, as a small child, he did not know that he had autism and only learned that he had special needs because everyone else said that he had them. Although he can read – even aloud – it is almost impossible for him to have a conversation. He can manage to speak a few words, but they are often the opposite of what he intends to say because "the words coming out of my mouth are the only ones I can access at the time."[161] He adds: "Even with straightforward 'Yes' or 'No' questions, we make mistakes. It happens all the time to me that the other person misunderstands or misinterprets what I've just said."[162]

The book is written in a question and answer format. As such, this is a very different kind of pathography. The first question asks how he is able to write. He responds that his mother invented an alphabet grid that works with his computer. Using it, Higashida states that he can express his "true self."[163] The second question asks why people with autism speak "loudly" and "weirdly," and he responds that this is unintentional, something that he and many others are not able to control.

The third question asks why people with autism repeat the same questions over and over. He responds by saying this seems to be related to how his memory works: "my way of remembering [is different] from everyone else's. I imagine a normal person's memory is arranged continuously, like a line. My memory, however, is more like a pool of dots. I'm always 'picking up' these dots – by asking my questions – so I can arrive back at the memory that the dots represent."[164] Although he recognizes his verbal communication difficulties, he usually understands quite well and he dislikes it when people address him as if he were a child; it makes him feel as though he has been written off with "zero chance of a decent future."[165] He adds that his memory differences result in behavioral issues, as people with autism often do things they are not supposed to do simply because they have forgotten that they are not supposed to do them. Consequently, they experience considerable shame for this routine forgetting.

Higashida addresses a number of questions commonly associated with autism, pointing out which ones apply to his own experience and which do not. For example, Question 16 asks, why do persons with autism not like being touched? He answers by acknowledging that although this is the case for others, he does not mind being touched. Question 31 asks why persons with autism are picky eaters, and, again, he notes that he does not have this problem but that he can understand why others might. His guess is that it just takes longer for persons with autism to learn to appreciate new foods because of tastes and textures.

Question 20 asks why he makes "a huge fuss" over small mistakes. He acknowledges that this is not something that he wants to do but that his mind just shuts down. He adds that it is very difficult – almost impossible – for him to control his emotions, and that he often just needs to leave or get out of the situation. When he observes the social effects of his emotional outbursts, he writes: "I hate myself. I just hate myself."[166] A few pages later he writes:

"You can't begin to imagine how miserable and sad we get."[167] Still, when he was asked what I have called *The Jamison Question* (Would you like to be "normal"?), he answers, "no," because he does not know what that would be like. Instead, he thinks the task is to learn to love himself as he is.[168]

Question 25 is the title of the book: What is the reason you jump? He writes: "When I'm jumping, it's as if my feelings are going upward to the sky. Really, my urge to be swallowed up by the sky is enough to make my heart quiver. When I'm jumping, I can feel my body parts really well, too . . . and that makes me feel so, so good."[169] He adds that another reason that he jumps is to shake off emotions that make him feel constrained: "I'm shaking loose the ropes that are tying up my body."[170]

According to Higashida, perception can be a positive feature of autism: "When you see an object, it seems that you see it as an entire thing first, and only afterward do its details follow on. But for people with autism, the details jump straight out at us first of all, and then only gradually, detail by detail, does the whole image sort of float up into focus."[171] He adds, "People with autism get to cherish this beauty, as if it's a kind of blessing to us."[172]

When Higashida is asked why persons with autism like to line things up, he confirms that this is the case for him, but he does not give a clear explanation as to why, other than it's just fun. Likewise, he notes that persons with autism like repetition very much – be it television commercials, music, stories, and so forth – and he suggests that this is because they can guess what is going to happen next. Persons with autism also often like numbers because they are unchanging, simple, clear, and predictable. Upon reflection, he adds that repetition is sometimes experienced as involuntary, "like our brains keep sending out the same order, time and again. Then, while we are repeating the action, we get to feel really good and incredibly comforted."[173]

10.2 Clinical Information

Autism spectrum disorder has five key diagnostic criteria. These include the following:

1. Difficulty in social communication and interaction (e.g., social–emotional reciprocity, nonverbal communication, and relationships)
2. Repetitive patterns, interests, and activities (e.g., lining up toys, inflexible routines, or hypersensitivity to environment: temperature, texture, etc.)
3. Symptoms must appear in early development
4. Symptoms must cause significant impairment and/or distress

5. The symptoms must not be better explained by another diagnosis, such as an intellectual disability[174]

The *DSM-5* noted that previous diagnoses of autistic disorder, Asperger's disorder, and pervasive development disorder not otherwise specified (in the *DSM-IV*) should be replaced with this diagnosis,[175] which the *DSM-5-TR* reaffirmed.[176] A key reason for the change is that "manifestations of the disorder also vary greatly … hence, the term *spectrum*."[177] This is clearly an advance from the thinking in the 1940s when so-called refrigerator mothers were blamed for "causing" autism by being "too cold" to their children.[178] The *DSM-5-TR* also lists several specifiers: intellectual impairment; language impairment; other known medical conditions; other neurodevelopmental, mental, or behavioral problems; and with or without catatonia.

Recently, the term "profound autism" has been adopted to indicate a state beyond "severe." Advocates for persons with autism spectrum disorder have pointed out that an unintended side effect of portraying these patients in such a positive light on television and in movies has had the effect of the public taking the disorder less seriously. This can lead to a reduction of resources, accommodations, and so forth.[179]

Perhaps the most poignant clinical criterion Higashida describes is his difficulty with relationships. He explains that people sometimes assume that he wants to be left alone but, in fact, persons with autism love being with other people: "But because things never, ever go right, we end up getting used to being alone, without even noticing this is happening," and, sadly, he adds: "I end up feeling miserable and ashamed that I can't manage a proper human relationship."[180] For this reason, he says that persons with autism often like nature, walking, trees, and water – these things tend to make persons with autism feel connected to life, especially when social life is often so very difficult.

In an introduction to the book, David Mitchell writes that this book gives us "proof that locked inside the helpless-seeming autistic body is a mind as curious, subtle, and complex as yours, as mine, as anyone's," and that, while outside observers often assume that persons with autism cannot experience empathy, this is just not the case, for "both emotional poverty and an aversion to company are not *symptoms* of autism but *consequences* of autism."[181] This is underscored by the fact that Higashida ends the book with a fictional short story about what it is like to be unseen. The story is a remarkable piece of writing in-and-of-itself, but it is especially illuminating because it demonstrates the rich creative inner life of persons with autism – they *are* capable of empathy – and they also desire social connections even if they have difficulty establishing and maintaining them.

11 Eating Disorders

11.1 Wasted

In *Wasted*, Marya Hornbacher tells of her experience suffering from both anorexia nervosa and bulimia. She became bulimic at the age of nine, throwing up daily until the age of twelve, and then multiple times a day afterward. She notes that she first began simply out of curiosity. By age fifteen, Hornbacher became anorexic. This pathography details the progression of her illness, and her recovery, but, most interestingly, it wrestles deeply with its meaning: What are eating disorders *really* about? Her answers to this question are woven throughout the text.

During the course of these eating disorders, Hornbacher was hospitalized six times, explaining that, at the time of writing, a starvation diet was considered to be 900 calories a day and that she was eating 320.[182] About the effects of such a diet, she writes: "Starvation does eventually hit the brain. First it eats all your fat. Then it eats your exoskeletal muscles. Then it eats your internal organs, one of which is the brain."[183] At her lowest point, her weight was fifty-two pounds.[184] She laments being so stereotypically common: a young, White, middle-class female with an eating disorder. She wrote the book because "I believe some people will recognize themselves in it – eating disordered or not – and because I believe, perhaps naively, that they might be willing to change their own behavior, get help if they need it, entertain the notion that their bodies are acceptable."[185]

Why does one suffer from an eating disorder? To the common answer of "control," she says that it is more complex and existential than that, for eating disorders also are about: "History, philosophy, society, personal strangeness, family fuck-ups, autoerotics, myth, mirrors, love and death and S & M, magazines and religion, the individual's blind-folded stumble walk through an ever-stranger world."[186] Although she agrees that eating disorders are an attempt to grab power, as well as to form an identity and to protest, she adds that, as an eating disorder progresses, it ceases to be about any one thing and it takes on a life of its own.[187]

Hornbacher further suggests that eating disorders are not only about vanity, immaturity, and madness, but they also are a form of addiction: "You become addicted to a number of their effects. The two most basic and important: the pure adrenaline that kicks in when you're starving – you're high as a kite, sleepless, full of a frenetic, unstable energy – and the heightened intensity of experience that eating disorders initially induce."[188] She goes on to say that no matter how much weight one loses, it is never enough – the worries do not cease.

Hornbacher identifies some other characteristics common among persons with eating disorders. They tend to be competitive, intelligent, and perfectionistic, excelling in school, athletics, and artistic pursuits. She adds: "We also tend to quit without warning. Refuse to go to school, drop out, quit jobs, leave lovers, move, lose all our money. We get sick of being impressive."[189] She disagrees that eating disorders are about "stopping time" (i.e., puberty),[190] but she did feel that her eating disorder was "an apology" to her father for becoming a woman.

As a baby, Hornbacher recalls that her parents noted that she suffered from food allergies. Some of her earliest memories are of her parents making comments about food – what has salt, what has fat, what has sugar, and so forth. Her grandmother, too, would make disconcerting comments: "I remember my grandmother giving me toast and tea ... and then told me I'd get fat and whisked the toast out of reach."[191]

Although she feels as though she had a happy childhood, she remembers that her parents fought frequently and that her father showed her love by giving her food. Her mother, in contrast, was very thin and food-avoidant. At the end of eighth grade, a friend told a school counselor about her bulimia, which, rather than feeling betrayed, Hornbacher appreciated. When she told her mother that she was throwing up, her mother responded by saying that she used to do the same thing.

Both of Hornbacher's parents were affiliated with the theater, so appearances and costumes became a central part of their family life. This affected how she saw her body: she felt it was a costume that she could change. She comments that culture in the United States associates thinness with wealth and success, while fatness is associated with weakness and poverty. Being fit takes time, which requires money. Thus, being thin and beautiful is a means of portraying one's social and economic status.

Hornbacher suggests that bulimia is sometimes hard to detect because the person eats normally in the presence of others, binging and purging in secret, while, at the same time, maintaining an average weight. A doctor, for example, once said to her, "Well, it's not like you're a sixty-pound anorectic or anything."[192] Likewise, someone's boyfriend once said she looked like a model.[193] Consequently, her behavior, when problematic, was either not recognized, even by a professional, or it was praised: "Unless you are so emaciated that you can barely walk," she writes, "people don't think you 'look' anorexic."[194]

Hornbacher points out that often there are comorbidities with eating disorders, such as obsessive-compulsive disorder or depression. She adds that people with eating disorders often have a conflicted relationship with sex, sometimes avoiding it altogether, other times engaging in sexual activities without much forethought. By her own account, Hornbacher notes that she became sexually promiscuous at the age of thirteen, when she also began experimenting with drugs (including using needles) and alcohol. At fourteen, she had an unplanned pregnancy, which ended in a miscarriage.

Hornbacher concludes her pathography by saying that, for her, writing the book was neither satisfying nor therapeutic. She regrets that her body has aged so considerably due to the way she mistreated it. In hindsight, she does not have a good reason for why or how she recovered: "I guess what happened was I got so tired of being so dull,"[195] and "I say it got boring, so I stopped."[196] She does add one striking piece of wisdom about life in general: "But in some ways, the most significant choices one makes in life are done for reasons that are not all that dramatic, not earth shaking at all – often enough, the choices we make are, for better or for worse, made by default."[197]

11.2 Clinical Information

There are three diagnostic criteria for anorexia nervosa:

1. Restriction of calorie intake such that it leads to a significantly low body weight
2. Intense fear of gaining weight
3. Disturbance in how one experiences one's weight or body[198]

There is a specifier as to whether the patient has engaged in episodes of binge eating or purging within the last three months. If not, this is a restricting type. If so, this is a binge eating/purging type (which Hornbacher demonstrated). The *DSM-5-TR* adds that cross-over behavior is not uncommon.[199] There is a second specifier that indicates whether the condition is in partial or full remission (if the patient was previously diagnosed) and a third specifier on severity (mild, moderate, severe, and extreme). Severity is measured by body mass index.[200] Although it is predominately women who suffer from this disorder,[201] a considerable number of gay men also suffer from this disorder,[202] and, to a much lesser extent, straight men. However, among adolescents rates may be similar, regardless of gender.[203]

A clinical issue that plays a major role in Hornbacher's pathography is the excessive fear of gaining weight and how this is manifested in terms of behavior. Hornbacher's pathography describes common tricks that bulimics develop, such as the use of "markers." A marker is when a patient eats a food that is easily identifiable (such as Doritos) so that, when the marker becomes visible in the vomit, the person can be sure everything has been regurgitated. Hornbacher would also vomit in the bathroom with the water running in order to mask sounds.

Other signs that someone has an eating disorder are when they eat unusual combinations of food or skip meals.[204] Excessive exercise can be a sign, too, as Hornbacher would run twenty-five miles a day. To shed weight, she would sometimes use ex-lax to induce bowel movements and ipecac to vomit. To fool nurses and doctors, she would use caffeine to boost her metabolism and heart rate, as well as decaffeinated drinks to retain fluids for body weight.[205] And she would hide weights in her pockets to rig the scale. What Hornbacher underscores with her secretive behaviors is that fear can be chronic rather than acute, more calculated and cerebral than an impulsive reaction to, say, a fire, bully, or bear. Morally, the deceptive behavior here is more about fear than lying, deserving our compassion rather than condemnation.

12 Key Personal Themes in Pathographies of Mental Illness

If the *DSM*, because it is empirically oriented and evidenced based, aims to produce generalizable knowledge (i.e., trends), the reading of pathographies can yield useful experiential insights. By reading a considerable number of pathographies together about different mental illnesses, certain key themes stand out, which differ from the empirical trends identified by scientific and medical researchers. Based on the pathographies presented here, seven personal themes are identified. Of course, other themes could be identified, both in these pathographies and in others not included in this Element, but the personal themes lifted up here are perennial issues in the field worthy of continued consideration.

1. The first personal theme is *The Jamison Question*. If a given mental illness could be prevented or cured, such that it never affected anyone ever again, should this step be taken? Jamison, as noted, gave a qualified "no" to this question (because medication works for her), feeling that her life has been richer and fuller on account of her experiences. Saks, directly addressing this question, felt that she would have liked to have been cured of schizophrenia, seeing no pleasure in her psychotic experiences because they are like waking nightmares. Higashida, despite his profound suffering and experiences of shame and isolation, would not want to be cured of autism, because this is the only life that he knows and he thinks that his goals are to accept himself more and to encourage society to be more accepting of neuro-atypical persons.

Although *The Jamison Question* is hypothetical today, it is conceivable that someday, given advances in gene editing, we will have to grapple with our collective answer. In contrast, if promising technological advances indicated that cancers could be prevented, such research would not generate similar moral debates in the medical community and various governments. There are other conditions where the answer is not as straightforward. The Deaf community, for example, has been concerned that medical advancements could lead to the elimination of their culture, which advocates want to preserve.[206] This is a fundamental question of value for the philosophy of medicine that needs to be negotiated. The whole field of disability studies is essential reading for making sense of these debates.[207] And Jamison remains a powerful voice for seeing the beauty of experience *with* profound mental illness: "Even when I have been my most psychotic . . . I have been aware of finding new corners in my mind and heart . . . [and] I cannot imagine becoming jaded to life, because I know of those limitless corners, with their limitless views."[208]

    2. The second personal theme might be called the issue of *The True Self.* Jamison, again, struggled with this issue, as she felt that when she was on medication she lost her identity. As a professor, it was very difficult for her to lose the ability to concentrate. On medication, she lost her creative insights as well. The question for many sufferers is: Is treatment making me more or less of myself? Other side effects – such as weight gain, the loss of libido, or the inability to orgasm – can have an impact on identity, affecting one's willingness to take medication. Jamison, too, weighs in on this question, when she says that "so many people who get depressed . . . [feel that their] depressions were more complicated and existentially based than they actually were."[209] But Jamison, after much struggle, came to realize that medication gave her back a self. In a different way, Nic Sheff felt that, by getting sober, he was no longer "cool," and so he relapsed a number of times, hesitant to give up such a large part of his sense of self. Treatment impacts the way people experience themselves, and those with mental illness need to sort through what this means for them.

    3. Relatedly, a third personal theme is the issue of *Disease* v. *Will.* It was especially helpful for David Sheff to view addiction as a disease so that he did not see his son as immoral. He quotes an addiction specialist who said: "I've studied alcohol, cocaine, methamphetamine, heroin, marijuana and more recently obesity. There's a pattern in compulsion. I've never come across a single person that was addicted that wanted to be addicted. Something has happened in their brains that has led to that process."[210] Nic, too, found this helpful, in that he did not regard himself as his true self when he was addicted (the second personal theme), doing things such as lying and stealing, seemingly against his will (the third personal theme). Clinically and therapeutically, it is a delicate balance to tease out how much to emphasize human agency when considering a particular mental illness or problem. Nic played some role in his addiction; but changes in brain chemistry due to drug use limited his ability to choose or resist certain behaviors and patterns of thinking. These kinds of issues

might apply to eating disorders, too, as Hornbacher made the case that they should be viewed as comparable to addictions. Saks also struggled with her role in accepting medication, feeling as though she should be able to beat her mental illness on her own. It was only when she surrendered her will that she was able to gain back her life.

4. A fourth personal theme is *Stigma*. Although applying to every form of mental illness, the pathographies presented here illustrate a variety of stigmas. A key purpose of Styron in writing *Darkness Visible* was to combat stigma surrounding suicide. In an important way, he contributed to a social shift of seeing mental illnesses as diseases like diabetes or cancer. In almost each of the memoirs, authors compare the stigma of their own mental illness with that of another. Kaysen, for instance, felt as though her diagnosis (borderline personality disorder) carried more stigma than, say, bipolar disease, for the simple reason that there was no medication that she could take to make her better. It was as though she were defective as a person. Likewise, there was considerable stigma surrounding the Klebolds and the Dahmers for the murders that their sons committed. Like addiction, choice – and thus moral fault – was involved and so the parents struggled with the question of responsibility. When a child does wrong, who is to blame?

This intersects with *The Jamison Question* in the sense that some mental illnesses (such as schizophrenia) may carry more stigma than others. Perhaps Saks, writing about schizophrenia, sums up stigma the best with this simple observation: "When you have cancer, people send flowers; when you lose your mind, they don't."[211]

5. A fifth personal theme is the issue of *Power and Knowledge*. Michel Foucault explores this issue in his books *The Birth of the Clinic*[212] and *Madness and Civilization*.[213] A significant book written by a psychiatrist in this regard is Thomas Szasz's *The Myth of Mental Illness*.[214] Foucault proposes that knowledge and power are always connected; things that appear to be neutral – such as scientific ideas – have values embedded in them that serve to support some over others. An example in the history of psychiatry is the removal of homosexuality as a psychiatric illness.[215] What was once considered to be sin was transformed into a medical illness, which then became simply a way of being. But the ones who decide the nomenclature are those with certain forms of power.

In the pathographies included in this Element, Kaysen forcefully raised this subject by addressing issues of sexism head-on. She notes that the *DSM* lists "inappropriately intense anger" as a criterion of her diagnosis, but, given all of the personal and social injustices she has experienced and witnessed, she asks: "What would have been an appropriate level of intensity for my anger at feeling shut out of life?"[216] In this respect, she seems to echo the anti-psychiatry movement, which owes so much to Foucault.

Similarly, Hornbacher addressed issues of sexism and misogyny in Western culture in a way that recalls Foucault's notion of subjectification (how persons make themselves into who they are).[217] Although people may believe their choices to be free, they may, in fact, be influenced by outside oppressive forces. Anorexia may be a case-in-point, Hornbacher suggests. In other words, if Western culture is fundamentally or deeply misogynistic, are eating disorders a predictable outcome, where women starve themselves literally to death?

Relatedly, issues of race and racism can be imbedded in psychiatric diagnoses. In medical humanities, a central book in this regard is Jonathan Metzl's *The Protest Psychosis*.[218] Metzl points out that, in the early twentieth century, schizophrenia was largely a disease that was diagnosed in White women but, as the century progressed, the clinical criteria were changed and Black men became increasingly diagnosed with schizophrenia. Women were often given this diagnosis when they had trouble completing their "wifely duties" (such as housecleaning and child-rearing) but Black men were given the diagnosis when they were actively involved in the Civil Rights movement. This is why Metzl titles his book *The Protest Psychosis*. During the Civil Rights era, psychiatric hospitals were another tool of the state to lock Black men away in a place other than prison. But Metzl's point is not that psychiatrists were overtly and intentionally racist (though some were). Rather, his point is that assumptions about race and racism become embedded in medical perception and clinical criteria such that individual doctors can be unaware of these structural dynamics.

6. A sixth personal theme is *Reliability*. As Hawkins observes, pathographies do not represent *the* truth. Rather than objectivity, they offer a perspective – one that is intentionally constructed and crafted over time, especially as they are intended for publication. Styron, for example, wrote with the agenda of destigmatizing suicide and also portraying the psychiatric hospital in a positive light. By narrating the story in such a way that he made the choice to go to the hospital, it is possible that he was trying to encourage others to do the same when they need such care. Or it could be that this was his emotional truth. In any case, it is very unlikely, as noted, that his hospitalization occurred in this way, given the description taken by his daughter documenting that night.

Kaysen, as noted, plays with time and chronology in her pathography, directly raising the question as to whether she is a reliable narrator in the chapter entitled: "Do you Believe Him or Me?"[219] She knows that, because she apparently suffers from a mental illness, she will not be believed, and thus she goes to great lengths to establish her reliability.

Sue Klebold, writing about her son, obviously was trying to rescue the memory of her son, both for herself and for him. Each writer has an agenda, which is implied or stated, and the reader is tasked with taking from these pathographies what seems useful. When friends or family members write their pathographies – after, for example, the sufferer dies (e.g., Jeffrey Dahmer, Dylan Klebold) – they are writing to make sense of their own lives, or trying to cope in some way, and this, of course, shapes our interpretation of "the case." The pathographies in this Element have been presented almost without comment, not on the basis of their veracity, but because of the insights they provide.

7. A seventh personal theme is *Hope*. Just as pathographies are typically painful, they often offer some degree of hope. Indeed, this is the whole point of Saks's pathography and her public talks: to inform people that a life with schizophrenia is not worthless. Klebold's book, too, is hopeful in its own way by advocating for brain health screening for children as a preventive measure against future massacres. Styron's book ends on a note of hope that even the worst depressions pass. Quoting Dante, he writes:

> *In the middle of the journey of our life*
> *I found myself in a dark wood,*
> *For I had lost the right path.*[220]

Those lines capture a metaphor for depression and other illnesses and crises, just as these lines, also from Dante, capture hope beautifully:

> *And so we came forth, and once again beheld the stars.*[221]

Perhaps the most important point to underscore is that hope is made possible and nurtured by means of social connections.[222] Without the love and care of friends, family members, and partners, it is unlikely that the persons with mental illness in these pathographies would have led their productive lives. Dahmer's isolation further illustrates this point. And, despite his profound difficulties with communication, Higoshida was able to find a way to connect with the world, which, ultimately, provides grounds for hope.

It is easy to ignore – and thus devalue – those we do not understand. An objective here is that, by reading these pathographies, persons with mental illness will be better understood and that we all might grow in empathetic awareness and relational connection.

Appendix: Further Reading

Core Texts of the Field

1. Anne Hawkins, *Reconstructing Illness*
2. Arthur Frank, *The Wounded Storyteller*
3. Bradley Lewis, *Narrative Psychiatry*
4. Craig LeCroy and Jane Holschuh, *First Person Accounts of Mental Illness and Recovery*
5. Vanessa Hazzard and Iresha Picot, eds., *The Color of Hope*

Depression

1. Alexandra Styron, *Reading My Father*
2. Meri Nana-Ama Danquah, *Willow Weep for Me*
3. Allie Brosh, *Solutions and Other Problems*
4. Kao Kalia Yang, "A Refugee Woman on Antidepressants"
5. David Foster Wallace, "The Depressed Person"
6. Peter Kramer, *Listening to Prozac*
7. Elizabeth Wurtzel, *Prozac Nation*
8. Nell Casey, ed., *Unholy Ghost*

Bipolar Illness

1. Kay Jamison, *Touched with Fire*
2. Elissa Washuta, *My Body Is a Book of Rules*
3. Thomas Cole, *No Color is My Kind*

Schizophrenia

1. Esme Wang, *The Collected Schizophrenias*
2. Jonathan Metzl, *The Protest Psychosis*
3. Sylvia Nasar, *A Beautiful Mind*

Addiction

1. Jeannette Walls, *The Glass Castle*
2. Augusten Burroughs, *Dry*

3. Nick Flynn, *Another Bullshit Night in Suck City*
4. Caroline Knapp, *Drinking: A Love Story*

Borderline Personality Disorder

1. Kiera Van Gelder, *The Buddha and the Borderline*
2. Marsha Linehan, *Building a Life Worth Living*
3. Tabetha Martin et al., *This Is Not the End*
4. Debbie Corso, *Stronger Than BPD*

Conduct Disorder, Psychopathy, and Antisocial Personality Disorder

1. Ralph Larkin, *Comprehending Columbine*
2. Lillyth Quillan, "The Isolating Life of Parenting a Potential Psychopath," *The Atlantic*
3. Lionel Shriver, *We Need to Talk about Kevin*
4. Lionel Dahmer, *A Father's Story*
5. Richard Tithecott, *Of Men and Monsters*

Autism Spectrum Disorder

1. Temple Grandin, *Thinking in Pictures*
2. Anand Prahlad, *The Secret Life of a Black Aspie*
3. Kristine Barnett, *The Spark: A Mother's Story of Nurturing, Genius, and Autism*

Eating Disorders

1. Stephanie Covington Armstrong, *Not All Black Girls Know How to Eat*
2. Harriet Brown, *Brave Girl Eating*
3. Natasha Holme, *Lesbian Crushes and Bulimia*

Notes

1. Cancer and neurological pathographies are the most numerous. See Kearney 2006, 111.
2. See, however, the introduction in this book: LeCroy & Holschuh 2012.
3. In this essay, the fifth edition of this text is indicated as follows: *DSM-5*. The most recent version of the manual is the *DSM-5-TR*.
4. Danquah 1998, 20.
5. Hawkins 1993.
6. Hawkins 1993, ix.
7. Czerwiec et al. 2015; Venkatesan & Saji 2018.
8. Sacks 1999.
9. Hawkins 1993, 177, note 1.
10. Sacks 1999, 229.
11. Hawkins 1993, ix–x.
12. Hawkins 1993, xii.
13. Hawkins 1993, xii.
14. Hawkins 1999.
15. She adds a fourth category, drawing on William James, which she calls healthy mindedness, but this category is not so much of a pattern as it is a value imbedded within the writing. These pathographies tend to advocate for "alternative" treatments. See James 2003.
16. Hawkins 1999.
17. Frank 2002.
18. Frank 1993, 249; Hawkins 1993, 13.
19. Frank 1993, 252.
20. Frank 2019.
21. McEntyre 2011, 455.
22. McEntyre 2011, 455.
23. McEntyre 2011, 462.
24. McEntyre 2011, 462.
25. McEntyre 2011, 462.
26. McEntyre 2011, 462.
27. Charon & Montello 2002, ix.
28. Charon & Montello 2002, x.
29. Montello 2014, S3.
30. Styron 1992, 17.
31. Styron 1992, 50.
32. Styron 1992, 40.
33. Forman 1975.
34. Mangold 1999.
35. Hawkins 1993, 24.
36. Styron 2002, 133–134.
37. American Psychiatric Association 2022, 183.

38. American Psychiatric Association 2022, 183.
39. Jamison 1996, 5.
40. Jamison 1996, 5–6.
41. Jamison 1996, 97–98.
42. American Psychiatric Association 2022, 139.
43. American Psychiatric Association 2022, 140.
44. American Psychiatric Association 2022, 140.
45. American Psychiatric Association 2022, 148.
46. Jamison 1996, 217.
47. Jamison 1996, 218.
48. Rund 2009.
49. Vahabzadeh et al. 2011.
50. Appelbaum 2013.
51. Saks 2007, 8.
52. Saks 2007, 12–13.
53. Saks 2007, 13.
54. Saks 2007, 83.
55. Saks 2007, 84.
56. Saks 2007, 92.
57. Saks 2007, 92.
58. Freud 1989.
59. Saks 2007, 93.
60. Saks 2007, 335.
61. Saks 2007, 336.
62. Saks 2007, 336.
63. Saks 1985.
64. American Psychiatric Association 2022, 101–102.
65. American Psychiatric Association 2022, 113–114.
66. Zick et al. 2022.
67. Saks 2007, 124.
68. Saks 2007, 124.
69. Saks 2007, 124–125.
70. Saks 2007, 234.
71. Saks 2007, 234.
72. Sheff 2009a, 14.
73. Sheff 2009a, 15.
74. Sheff 2009a, 72.
75. Sheff 2009a, 81–82.
76. Evins et al. 2012.
77. Sheff 2009a, 88.
78. Sheff 2009a, 93.
79. Sheff 2009a, 138.
80. Sheff 2009a, 195.
81. Sheff 2009b, epigram.
82. Sheff 2009b, 159.
83. Sheff 2009b, 197.

84. Sheff 2009b, 5.
85. Sheff 2009b, 5.
86. Sheff 2009b, 5.
87. Sheff 2009b, 69.
88. Sheff 2009b, 36.
89. Sheff 2009b, 36.
90. Sheff 2009b, 142.
91. American Psychiatric Association 2022, 544.
92. American Psychiatric Association 2022, 553–554.
93. Sheff 2009b, 123.
94. Sheff 2009b, 123.
95. See, for example, Gregory 2004.
96. Kaysen 1994, 5.
97. Kaysen 1994, 6.
98. Kaysen 1994, 157.
99. Kaysen 1994, 166.
100. Kaysen 1994, 27.
101. Stone 2000.
102. Merrigan 2018.
103. Merrigan 2018.
104. Kaysen 1994, 59.
105. Kaysen 1994, 151.
106. Kaysen 1994, 18.
107. Kaysen 1994, 19.
108. Kaysen 1994, 36.
109. Kaysen 1994, 37.
110. Kaysen 1994, 150.
111. Kaysen 1994, 42.
112. Kaysen 1994, 167.
113. Kaysen 1994, 168.
114. American Psychiatric Association 2022, 752–753.
115. American Psychiatric Association 2013, 666.
116. American Psychiatric Association 2022, 755.
117. Erikson 1962, 99–104.
118. Kaysen 1994, 94.
119. Klebold 2016, ix.
120. Klebold 2016, 37.
121. Klebold 2016, 95.
122. Klebold 2016, 61.
123. Klebold 2016, 224, 226.
124. Klebold 2016, 78–79.
125. Klebold 2016, 93.
126. Klebold 2016, 101.
127. Klebold 2016, 171.
128. Klebold 2016, 172.
129. Klebold 2016, 206.

130. Klebold 2016, 134.
131. Klebold 2016, 132.
132. Klebold 2016, 136.
133. Klebold 2016, 136.
134. Klebold 2016, 236–237.
135. Klebold 2016, 237.
136. Klebold 2016, 200.
137. American Psychiatric Association 2022, 521.
138. American Psychiatric Association 2022, 531.
139. American Psychiatric Association 2022, 531.
140. American Psychiatric Association 2013, 470–472, 474.
141. American Psychiatric Association 2022, 535.
142. Klebold 2016, 161.
143. Tithecott 1997.
144. See, for example, Meyers 2017.
145. Oates 2009.
146. Ratcliff 2006.
147. Backderf 2012.
148. Martens & Palermo 2005.
149. Backderf 2012, 11.
150. Backderf 2012, 23.
151. Backderf 2012, 60.
152. Backderf 2012, 87.
153. Backderf 2012, 127.
154. Martens & Palermo 2005, 301.
155. American Psychiatric Association 2022, 748.
156. American Psychiatric Association 2022, 748.
157. American Psychiatric Association 2022, 748.
158. American Psychiatric Association 2022, 749–750.
159. American Psychiatric Association 2022, 751.
160. American Psychiatric Association 2013, 663.
161. Higashida 2016, 17.
162. Higashida 2016, 19.
163. Higashida 2016, 6.
164. Higashida 2016, 10.
165. Higashida 2016, 15.
166. Higashida 2016, 38.
167. Higashida 2016, 43.
168. Higashida 2016, 45.
169. Higashida 2016, 47.
170. Higashida 2016, 48.
171. Higashida 2016, 59.
172. Higashida 2016, 60.
173. Higashida 2016, 97.
174. American Psychiatric Association 2022, 56–57.
175. American Psychiatric Association 2013, 51.

176. American Psychiatric Association 2022, 57.
177. American Psychiatric Association 2022, 60.
178. Rudy 2021.
179. Leadbitter et al. 2021; McKinney et al. 2021.
180. Higashida 2016, 27, 29.
181. Higashida 2016, xv.
182. Hornbacher 2006, 247.
183. Hornbacher 2006, 257.
184. Hornbacher 2006, 2.
185. Hornbacher 2006, 5.
186. Hornbacher 2006, 4.
187. Hornbacher 2006, 64.
188. Hornbacher 2006, 105.
189. Hornbacher 2006, 136.
190. Hornbacher 2006, 229.
191. Hornbacher 2006, 33.
192. Hornbacher 2006, 178.
193. Hornbacher 2006, 182.
194. Hornbacher 2006, 242.
195. Hornbacher 2006, 278.
196. Hornbacher 2006, 280.
197. Hornbacher 2006, 280.
198. American Psychiatric Association 2022, 381.
199. American Psychiatric Association 2022, 382.
200. American Psychiatric Association 2022, 381.
201. American Psychiatric Association 2022, 384.
202. Morgan-Sowada & Gamboni 2021.
203. American Psychiatric Association 2022, 384.
204. Hornbacher 2006, 107.
205. Hornbacher 2006, 146.
206. Tucker 1998.
207. Garland-Thompson 2016.
208. Jamison 1996, 219.
209. Jamison 1996, 54.
210. Sheff 2009a, 180.
211. Saks 2007, 312.
212. Foucault 2012.
213. Foucault 2003.
214. Szasz 2010.
215. Glass 2002.
216. Kaysen 1994, 156.
217. Cole et al. 2015, 264–266.
218. Metzl 2009.
219. Kaysen 1994, 71.
220. Styron 1992, 83.
221. Styron 1992, 84.
222. Capps 2005.

References

American Psychiatric Association. *Diagnostic and Statistical Manual of Mental Disorders*, 5th ed. Washington, DC: American Psychiatric Association, 2013.

American Psychiatric Association. *Diagnostic and Statistical Manual of Mental Disorders*, 5th ed., Text Revision. Washington, DC: American Psychiatric Association, 2022.

Appelbaum, Paul. Public Safety, Mental Disorders, and Guns. *JAMA Psychiatry* 70 (2013): 565–566.

Backderf, Derf. *My Friend Dahmer*. New York: Abrams, 2012.

Busch, Fredric, and Sandberg, Larry. *Psychotherapy and Medication: The Challenge of Integration*. London: Routledge, 2016.

Capps, Donald. *Fragile Connections: Memoirs of Mental Illness for Pastoral Care Professionals*. St. Louis, MO: Chalice, 2005.

Charon, Rita, and Montello, Martha, eds. *Stories Matter: The Role of Narrative in Medical Ethics*. London: Routledge, 2002.

Cole, Thomas, Carlin, Nathan, and Carson, Ronald. *Medical Humanities: An Introduction*. New York: Cambridge University Press, 2015.

Czerwiec, MK, Williams, Ian, Squier, Susan et al. *Graphic Medicine Manifesto*. University Park, PA: Penn State University Press, 2015.

Erikson, Erik. *Young Man Luther: A Study in Psychoanalysis and History*. New York: WW Norton, 1962.

Evins, A. Eden, Green, Alan, Kane, John, and Murray, Robin. The Effect of Marijuana Use on the Risk for Schizophrenia. *The Journal of Clinical Psychiatry* 73 (2012): 1463–1468.

Forman, Miloš. *One Flew Over the Cuckoo's Nest* [motion picture]. Hollywood, CA: Fantasy Films/United Artists, 1975.

Foucault, Michel. *The Birth of the Clinic*. New York: Routledge, 2012.

Foucault, Michel. *Madness and Civilization*. New York: Routledge, 2003.

Frank, Arthur. *Review of Reconstructing Illness: Studies in Pathography. Literature and Medicine* 12 (1993): 248–252.

Frank, Arthur. *At the Will of the Body: Reflections on Illness*. Boston, MA: Houghton Mifflin Harcourt, 2002.

Frank, Arthur. Not Whether but How: Considerations on the Ethics of Telling Patients' Stories. *Hastings Center Report* 49 (2019): 13–16.

Freud, Sigmund. *On Dreams*. New York: WW Norton, 1989.

Garland-Thompson, Rosemarie. Becoming Disabled. *New York Times*, August 19, 2016. www.nytimes.com/2016/08/21/opinion/sunday/becoming-disabled.html.

Glass, Ira. 81 Words. *This American Life*, January 18, 2002. https://www
.thisamericanlife.org/204/81-words.

Gregory, Julie. *Sickened: The True Story of a Lost Childhood*. New York:
Bantam, 2004.

Hawkins, Anne. Pathography: Patient Narratives of Illness. *Western Journal of
Medicine* 171 (1999): 127–129.

Hawkins, Anne. *Reconstructing Illness: Studies in Pathography*. West
Lafayette, IN: Purdue University Press, 1993.

Higashida, Naoki. *The Reason I Jump: The Inner Voice of a Thirteen-Year-Old
Boy with Autism*. New York: Random House, 2016.

Hornbacher, Marya. *Wasted: A Memoir of Anorexia and Bulimia*. New York:
Harper Collins, 2006.

James, William. *The Varieties of Religious Experience: A Study in Human
Nature*. London: Routledge, 2003.

Jamison, Kay. *An Unquiet Mind: A Memoir of Moods and Madness*. New York:
Vintage, 1996.

Kaysen, Susanna. *Girl, Interrupted*. New York: Vintage, 1994.

Kearney, Peter. Autopathography and Humane Medicine: The Diving Bell and
the Butterfly – An Interpretation. *Medical Humanities* 32 (2006): 111–113.

Klebold, Sue. *A Mother's Reckoning: Living in the Aftermath of Tragedy*.
New York: Crown, 2016.

Leadbitter, Kathy, Buckle, Karen, Ellis, Ceri, and Dekker, Martijn. Autistic
Self-Advocacy and the Neurodiversity Movement: Implications for Autism
Early Intervention Research and Practice. *Frontiers in Psychology* (2021).
https://doi.org/10.3389/fpsyg.2021.635690.

LeCroy, Craig, and Holschuh, Jane, eds. *First Person Accounts of Mental
Illness and Recovery*. Hoboken, NJ: John Wiley, 2012.

Mangold, James. *Girl, Interrupted* [motion picture]. Hollywood, CA: Columbia
Pictures, 1999.

Martens, Willem, and Palermo, George. Loneliness and Associated Violent
Antisocial Behavior: Analysis of the Case Reports of Jeffrey Dahmer and
Dennis Nilsen. *International Journal of Offender Therapy and Comparative
Criminology* 49 (2005): 298–307.

McEntyre, Marilyn. Patient Poets: Pathography in Poetry. *Literature Compass* 8
(2011): 455–463.

McKinney, Ailbhe, Weisblatt, Emma, Hotson, Kathryn et al. Overcoming Hurdles
to Intervention Studies with Autistic Children with Profound Communication
Difficulties and Their Families. *Autism* 25 (2021): 1627–1639.

Merrigan, Tara. *Girl, Interrupted*, Twenty-Five Years Later. *The Paris Review*, June 27, 2018. https://www.theparisreview.org/blog/2018/06/27/girl-interrupted-twenty-five-years-later/.

Meri, Nana-Ama Danquah. *Willow Weep for Me: A Black Woman's Journey Through Depression*. New York: W. W. Norton, 1998.

Metzl, Jonathan. *The Protest Psychosis: How Schizophrenia Became a Black Disease*. Boston, MA: Beacon Press, 2009.

Meyers, Marc. *My Friend Dahmer* [motion picture]. Hollywood, CA: Attic Light Films, 2017.

Montello, Martha. Narrative Ethics. *Hastings Center Report* 44 (2014): S2–S6.

Morgan-Sowada, Heather, and Gamboni, Casey. Needing to Be "Perfect" to Be Loved: The Intersection of Body Dysmorphic Disorder, Sexual Identity, and Gay Culture in Gay Men. A Qualitative Study. *Sexual and Relationship Therapy* (2021). https://doi.org/10.1080/14681994.2021.1975672.

Oates, Joyce. *Zombie*. New York: Harper Collins, 2009.

Ratcliff, Roy. *Dark Journey Deep Grace: Jeffrey Dahmer's Story of Faith*. Abilene, TX: Leaf Wood, 2006.

Rudy, Lisa. Why "Refrigerator" Mothers Were Blamed for Autism. *VeryWell health*, January 25, 2021. www.verywellhealth.com/why-refrigerator-mothers-were-blamed-for-autism-260135.

Rund, Bjørn. Is Schizophrenia a Neurodegenerative Disorder? *Nordic Journal of Psychiatry* 63 (2009): 196–201.

Sacks, Oliver. *Awakenings*. New York: Vintage, 1999.

Saks, Eyln. *The Center Cannot Hold: My Journey through Madness*. New York: Hyperion, 2007.

Saks, Eyln. The Use of Mechanical Restraints in Psychiatric Hospitals. *Yale Law Journal* 95 (1985): 1836–1856.

Sheff, David. *Beautiful Boy: A Father's Journey through His Son's Addiction*. Boston, MA: Houghton Mifflin Harcourt, 2009a.

Sheff, Nic. *Tweak: Growing up on Methamphetamines*. New York: Atheneum, 2009b.

Stone, Alan. Split Personality. *Boston Review*, June 1, 2000. https://bostonreview.net/articles/alan-stone-split-personality/.

Styron, Rose. Strands. In *Unholy Ghost: Writers on Depression*. New York: Perennial, 2002.

Styron, William. Nell, Casey ed. *Darkness Visible: A Memoir of Madness*. New York: Vintage, 1992, pp. 126–137.

Szasz, Thomas. *The Myth of Mental Illness: Foundations of a Theory of Personal Conduct*. New York: Harper Perennial, 2010.

Tithecott, Richard. *Of Men and Monsters: Jeffrey Dahmer and the Construction of the Serial Killer.* Madison, WI: University of Wisconsin Press, 1997.

Tucker, Bonnie. Deaf Culture, Cochlear Implants, and Elective Disability. *Hastings Center Report* 28 (1998): 6–14.

Vahabzadeh, Arshya, Wittenauer, Justine, and Carr, Erika. Stigma, Schizophrenia and the Media: Exploring Changes in the Reporting of Schizophrenia in Major US Newspapers. *Journal of Psychiatric Practice* 17 (2011): 439–446.

Venkatesan, Sathyaraj, and Saji, Sweetha. Graphic Medicine and the Limits of Biostatistics. *AMA Journal of Ethics* 20 (2018): 897–901.

Zick, Jennifer, Staglin, Brandon, and Vinogradov, Sophia. Eliminate Schizophrenia. *Schizophrenia Research* 242 (2022): 147–149.

Acknowledgments

Many people provided feedback on this Element, or material related to this Element, over the years. I would like to thank my colleagues in the McGovern Center for Humanities and Ethics: Thomas Cole, Rebecca Lunstroth, Keisha Ray, Anson Koshy, Renee Flores, Deborah Franklin, Mary Horton, Alma Rosas, and Angela Polczynski. And I would like to thank a number of students who took a seminar on this topic with me. I learned a lot from our discussions. In particular, I would like to thank Amanda Actor, Breanna Alonzo, Lauren Beck, Rachel Beck, Jonathan Carroll, Aditi Chalise, Karen Cuartas, Christina Danna, Margaret Garrett, Kira Gomez, Himanshu Gupta, Maryam Haider, Anam Haque, Andrea Hernandez, Alexander Hunt, Jess Laney, Morgan Lynch, Ashlyn Manley, John McCarthy, Madison Meek, Amy Mullikin, Trisha Mulamreddy, Margaret O'Brien, Erin Orozco, Aashini Patel, Luan Phan, William Rieger, Jasper Shei, Sydne Steward, Will Tanigaki, Gabrielle Taper, Keziah Thomas, Kehan Vohra, and Jeffrey Woods. Finally, I would like to dedicate this essay to Vineeth John, a psychiatrist with a humanist's heart. I have been enriched by his friendship, humor, imagination, and insights.

Cambridge Elements ≡

Bioethics and Neuroethics

Thomasine Kushner
California Pacific Medical Center, San Francisco

Thomasine Kushner, PhD, is the founding Editor of the *Cambridge Quarterly of Healthcare Ethics* and coordinates the International Bioethics Retreat, where bioethicists share their current research projects, the Cambridge Consortium for Bioethics Education, a growing network of global bioethics educators, and the Cambridge-ICM Neuroethics Network, which provides a setting for leading brain scientists and ethicists to learn from each other.

About the Series

Bioethics and neuroethics play pivotal roles in today's debates in philosophy, science, law, and health policy. With the rapid growth of scientific and technological advances, their importance will only increase. This series provides focused and comprehensive coverage in both disciplines consisting of foundational topics, current subjects under discussion and views toward future developments.

Bioethics and Neuroethics

Elements in the Series

The Ethics of Consciousness
Walter Glannon

Responsibility for Health
Sven Ove Hansson

Roles of Justice in Bioethics
Matti Hayry

Bioethics, Public Reason, and Religion
Leonard M. Fleck

Controlling Love: The Ethics and Desirability of Using 'Love Drugs'
Peter Herissone-Kelly

Pathographies of Mental Illness
Nathan Carlin

A full series listing is available at: www.cambridge.org/EBAN